A Handbook for Those Already Born Study Guide Paperback

Greg Kuhn

Copyright © 2023 by Greg Kuhn

All rights reserved.

No portion of this book may be reproduced in any form without written permission from the publisher or author, except as permitted by U.S. copyright law.

Contents

Introduction	XI
1. Study Guide for the Introduction and Chapter 1: Who I Am and Who You Are	1
Section 1: Understanding the Quantum Field and Your True Nature	
Section 2: Discovering Your Identity as Energy-You	
Section 3: Embracing Your Authority as Energy-You	
Section 4: Understanding the Eternal Nature of Energy-You	
Section 5: Embracing Your Life's Purpose	
Section 6: Manifesting and Engaging with Reality Intentionally	
Section 7: Self Discovery and Unraveling Your True Self	
Section 8: Taking Charge of Your Journey	
Final Thoughts: The Quantum Field's Message to You	
2. Study Guide for Chapter 2: What Your Self Is	9
Section 1: Understanding Your Self and Its Collaborators	
Section 2: Leadership of Your Self	
Section 3: The Power of Your Body and Brain	
Section 4: Understanding Your Reality and Its Impact	
Section 5: Nurturing Your Self and Its Collaborators	
Section 6: Embracing Pain and Growth	

Section 7: Integrating Leadership Into Your Life
Section 8: Review and Continuing Growth
Conclusion

3. Study Guide for Chapter 3: How You Manifest and Engage With Your Reality   19

    Section 1: Understanding Consciousness and Reality
    Section 2: The Mechanics of Manifesting
    Section 3: How Real Is Your Reality?
    Section 4: An Atom Is Nothing
    Section 5: Manifesting Is Making Nothing Into Something
    Section 6: Manifesting Your Reality With Your Subconscious Mind
    Section 7: Your Beliefs' Perfect Storage Place
    Section 8: Manifesting Your Reality With Your Subconscious Mind
    Conclusion

4. Study Guide for Chapter 5: How to Intentionally Manifest Your Reality   25

    Instructions:
    Section One: Introduction to Intentional Manifesting
    Section Two: Understanding Your Emotional Perspective
    Section Three: Moving Toward Alignment
    Section Four: Overcoming Resistance
    Section Five: Embracing Patience and Persistence
    Section Six: The Journey to the Top
    Section 7: Implementing Belief-Raising in Other Areas
    Section 8: Reflecting on Your Journey
    Conclusion

5. Study Guide for Chapter 6: How to Intentionally Engage with   33
Your Reality
    Section 1: Introduction to Vibrational Alignment
    Section 2: Morning Journaling for Vibrational Alignment
    Section 3: Aligning with Opportunities, Not Outcomes
    Section 4: Aligning Under Any Circumstances
    Section 5: Taking Control of What's in Your Control
    Section 6: Correlation and Communication
    Section 7: Alignment on Challenging Days
    Section 8: Making Vibrational Alignment a Habit
    Conclusion

6. Study Guide for Chapter 7, Technique 1: Give Your Best Effort   41
to Follow Form
    Section 1: Introduction to Following Form
    Section 2: Identifying the Right Form
    Section 3: Adopting the Form
    Section 4: Understanding the Benefits
    Section 5: Dealing with Challenges and Setbacks
    Section 6: Cultivating Self-Compassion
    Section 7: Tracking Progress and Celebrating Success
    Section 8: Making Following Form a Way of Life
    Conclusion

7. Study Guide for Chapter 7, Technique 2: Satisfy Your Critic   49
    Section 1: Introduction to Satisfying Your Critic
    Section 2: Understanding the Concept of Satisfying Your Critic
    Section 3: Identifying Your Critics

Section 4: The Process of Satisfying Your Critic
Section 5: Overcoming Challenges and Internal Obstacles
Section 6: Building Transparent Accountability
Section 7: Embracing Feedback for Growth
Section 8: Integrating Satisfying Your Critic as a Habit
Conclusion

8. Study Guide for Chapter 7, Technique 3: Use Your Board of Directors — 57
    Section 1: Introduction to Using Your Board of Directors
    Section 2: Understanding the Concept of Using Your Board of Directors
    Section 3: Identifying Your Board Members
    Section 4: Establishing a Transparent Board Relationship
    Section 5: Leveraging Your Board's Expertise
    Section 6: Embracing Accountability and Growth
    Section 7: Adapting and Expanding Your Board
    Section 8: Integrating the Board of Directors Approach
    Conclusion

9. Study Guide for Chapter 7, Technique 4: Create a Positive Checkmate — 65
    Section 1: Introduction to Creating a Positive Checkmate
    Section 2: Understanding the Concept of Creating a Positive Checkmate
    Section 3: Identifying Key Allies
    Section 4: Establishing Transparency and Accountability
    Section 5: Embracing Challenges and Obstacles
    Section 6: Utilizing the Power of Connection
    Section 7: Deepening Relationships Through Accountability

Section 8: Integrating the Positive Checkmate Approach
Conclusion

10. Study Guide for Chapter 7, Technique 5: Manifest a Penny   71
    Section 1: Introduction to Manifesting a Penny
    Section 2: Understanding the Concept of Manifesting a Penny
    Section 3: Intentionally Manifesting a Penny
    Section 4: Engaging with the Penny's Energy
    Section 5: Expanding the Practice to Other Desires
    Section 6: Strengthening Manifesting Efficacy
    Section 7: Applying Manifesting Skills
    Section 8: Integrating Manifesting Skills
    Conclusion:

11. Study Guide for Chapter 7, Technique 6: Use a Positive Affirmation   79
    Section 1: Introduction to Positive Affirmations
    Section 2: Understanding Positive Affirmations
    Section 3: Crafting Effective Positive Affirmations
    Section 4: Implementing Positive Affirmations
    Section 5: Enhancing Affirmation Efficacy
    Section 6: Integrating Positive Affirmations into Challenging Situations
    Section 7: Expanding Positive Affirmations to Other Areas
    Section 8: Long-Term Affirmation Practice
    Conclusion:

12. Study Guide for Chapter 7, Technique 7: Make a Manifesting Mount Rushmore   87
    Section 1: Introduction to Making a Manifesting Mount Rushmore

Section 2: Understanding Making a Manifesting Mount Rushmore

Section 3: Identifying Desired States of Being

Section 4: Selecting Four Accomplishments

Section 5: Intentional Manifestation Techniques

Section 6: Collaborative Manifestation

Section 7: Balancing Responsibilities and Pressure

Section 8: Integrating Making a Manifesting Mount Rushmore into Daily Life

Conclusion:

13. Study Guide for Chapter 7, Technique 8: Create a Flow State   95

    Section 1: Introduction to Creating a Flow State

    Section 2: Understanding the Flow State

    Section 3: Selecting a Challenging Physical Activity

    Section 4: Creating Flow States through Practice

    Section 5: Recognizing Flow State Indicators

    Section 6: Processing Emotions in the Flow State

    Section 7: Direct Communication with the Quantum Field

    Section 8: Integrating Flow State in Daily Life

    Conclusion:

14. Study Guide for Chapter 8: How Greg Intentionally Manifests and Engages with His Reality   103

    Section 1: Reflecting on Opportunities

    Section 2: Identifying Limiting Beliefs

    Section 3: Embracing Responsibility for Fulfillment

    Section 4: Seeking Expert Mentorship

    Section 5: Applying the Metaphor of Running

Section 6: Mastering Each Step of Manifesting

Section 7: Recognizing Current Manifestation

Section 8: The Driving Force Behind Your Intentional Manifesting

Conclusion:

About the Author   113

Also By Greg Kuhn   115

INTRODUCTION

Welcome to "A Handbook for Those Already Born Study Guide." Within the pages of this guide, we embark on a transformative journey of self-discovery, intentional manifestation, and personal growth. As you delve into the profound concepts and practical techniques presented here, you will unlock the keys to manifesting a reality that aligns with your deepest desires and aspirations.

In the hustle and bustle of our daily lives, it is easy to lose sight of the immense power we hold within ourselves. Each one of us is bestowed with the ability to shape our reality, to create a life that resonates with our truest selves. The question is, how do we tap into this inherent potential? How do we shed the limitations that hold us back and unlock the path to a more fulfilling existence?

"A Handbook for Those Already Born", written by Greg Kuhn, addresses these fundamental questions and this study guide, based on that book, provides you with the tools, insights, and strategies to intentionally manifest a reality that reflects your innermost dreams. Drawing on timeless wisdom and cutting-edge research, this study guide offers a comprehensive roadmap to navigate a journey of personal transformation.

This guide does not merely present theories and concepts. To ensure the highest quality instruction for the principles laid out in his book, Greg Kuhn has partnered with Dr. Matt Kingsley, a highly esteemed high school administrator and seasoned personal development coach. Dr. Kingsley brings his expertise in curriculum development, individualized learning, formative assessment, and personal development to bear in this guide.

Dr. Kingsley's passion for empowering individuals has driven him to coach people and run personal development programs since 2001. With a wealth of experience and a compassionate approach, Matt has helped countless individuals break free from self-imposed limitations and embrace their true potential.

As you engage with the teachings of "A Handbook for Those Already Born Study Guide," you have the opportunity to take the next step in your personal evolution through specialized, life-changing courses and one-on-one Intentional Manifesting coaching. Greg Kuhn and Dr. Kingsley are collaborating to create courses and coaching programs that provide you with personalized guidance, helping you integrate the book's principles even deeper into your unique circumstances and challenges.

Embark on a Journey of Transformation with Greg Kuhn and Dr. Matt Kingsley!

Are you ready to unlock your full potential and manifest a life of abundance, joy, and purpose? Look no further! Greg Kuhn and Dr. Matt Kingsley are thrilled to introduce you to our upcoming courses and coaching programs. Courses and programs that will empower you to become the conscious creator of your reality.

These courses and programs delve deep into the secrets of quantum physics, Intentional Manifesting, and the power of intention. They are expertly crafted to guide you through practical techniques, insights, and scientific principles that will revolutionize the way you approach life. Whether you're seeking to enhance your career, improve relationships, attract more money, or boost your well-being, our transformative courses and programs will illuminate the path to your dreams.

Imagine having two dedicated mentors by your side – Greg Kuhn and Dr. Matt Kingsley – guiding you through specialized manifesting courses and tailored coaching sessions. Our courses and programs will provide you with personalized strategies, accountability, and expert guidance to ensure your journey towards manifestation mastery is both successful and fulfilling. Get ready to harness the energy of the universe and unleash your potential in ways you never thought possible.

Don't miss out on the opportunity to be notified when our courses and coaching programs become available. Click the link below to sign up and stay updated on all the exciting details. The universe is ready to collaborate with you on a transformational journey and we can't wait to be part of your success story.

Greg Kuhn and Dr. Matt Kingsley invite you to join us in creating a reality that aligns with your deepest desires. By clicking the link and signing up, you're taking the first step towards a life of abundance, purpose, and fulfillment. Let's embark on this captivating journey together – your transformation awaits!

Visit this page to be notified of Greg and Matt's Intentional Manifesting courses and coaching programs: https://skilled-designer-5245.ck.page/c962ff78b6

Chapter One

Study Guide for the Introduction and Chapter 1: Who I Am and Who You Are

Instructions: Use the information provided in the Introduction and Chapter 1 to answer the following questions and complete the activities. Consider your own beliefs and experiences as you work through each section. Feel free to take notes or reflect on your responses.

Section 1: Understanding the Quantum Field and Your True Nature

- What are some of the names given to the Quantum Field, according to the information provided in the handbook?

- Describe the Quantum Field's characteristics based on the information given. How does it interact with material reality?

- Explain why the Quantum Field enjoys experiencing life through human beings.

- In what way is the author (Greg Kuhn) connected to the Quantum Field and how does he communicate its message in this handbook?

- Why is the Quantum Field considered a trustworthy and benevolent guide?

Section 2: Discovering Your Identity as Energy-You

- How does the handbook define "you" in the context of the Quantum Field? What is your true nature?

- Fill in the Blank: Energy-You has the authority to choose _____. Example: actions, ideas, attitudes, focus

- Why is it challenging to remember who you truly are while experiencing life on this earthly plane?

- Compare the relationship between the Quantum Field and you to that of an archipelago and its islands. What does this analogy represent?

- How does the Quantum Field view separateness and how is it a necessary part of the human experience?

- What is the ultimate destiny of Energy-You after your time in the earthly world comes to an end?

- <u>Writing Exercise:</u> Share an example from your life when you consciously influenced your reality through your actions, ideas, attitudes, or focus. How did this experience demonstrate your role as Energy-You?

Section 3: Embracing Your Authority as Energy-You

- Explain the concept of energy in the context of material reality and the human body. How does it contribute to the feeling of solidity?

- Describe Energy-You's role in experiencing human life and how it influences your thoughts and actions.

- True or False: The separateness you experience in the material world is a necessary aspect of being human.

  - a) True

  - b) False

- What opportunities does Energy-You have to influence your life, and why is it essential to make conscious choices?

- Discuss how your actions, ideas, attitudes, and focus can impact not only your life but the lives of others as well.

- How does Greg Kuhn encourage you to manifest fulfilling outcomes and why is it essential to do so during your time on Earth?

- Reflection: How does the understanding that you and the Quantum Field are not actually separate on a quantum level affect your perspective on your connection to others and the world around you?

Section 4: Understanding the Eternal Nature of Energy-You

- How does the concept of eternal energy apply to both the Quantum Field and you as Energy-You?

- What happens to Energy-You immediately after your physical body dies and how does consciousness continue?

- Describe the characteristics of your next life after death and how it relates to your previous experiences.

- Explain how the choices you make in this life can influence your future experiences as Energy-You.

- Discuss the purpose of your current journey and how it contributes to the overall experience of the Quantum Field.

- <u>Activity:</u> Imagine your next life, where you can manifest anything from your previous reality. Create a list of three things or experiences you would manifest in that life. How do these desires align with your current journey as Energy-You?

Section 5: Embracing Your Life's Purpose

- State the primary purpose of your life, according to the handbook.

- Why did you come to this earthly plane and what opportunities does it provide for the Quantum Field?

- Describe the importance of giving your best effort to manifest reality as you desire.

- How does your ability to influence your life contribute to your growth and fulfillment?

- Discuss the relationship between the fulfillment of your journey and the fulfillment of the Quantum Field.

- Action Plan: Choose one strategy from the previous question and outline three specific steps you will take to incorporate it into your daily life. Consider any challenges you might face and how you will overcome them.

Section 6: Manifesting and Engaging with Reality Intentionally

- What is the main focus of this handbook and how does it aim to help you in your life's journey?

- Explain how your inherent ability to manifest and engage with reality is crucial for living a fulfilling life.

- Why is it important to dare to dream and manifest your desires during your time on Earth?

- Discuss how challenges in life present opportunities for growth and fulfillment.

- How does Greg Kuhn express his support and encouragement for you throughout this handbook?

- Brainstorming: List three strategies or practices you can implement to engage with reality more intentionally and manifest your desires. Consider actions, habits, or mindset shifts that can support your journey as Energy-You.

Section 7: Self Discovery and Unraveling Your True Self

- How does the handbook describe your self? What is its relationship with Energy-You?

- What role does the decider play in your life and how does it lead your self?

- Why is your journey constantly providing opportunities for growth and leadership?

- How does your self differ from the Quantum Field and how can you align them to live more intentionally?

- Discuss the potential for fulfillment as you manifest a successful life.

- <u>Reflective Writing:</u> Describe your aspirations for making the most of your time on Earth. What experiences, achievements, or personal growth do you hope to manifest during your journey?

Section 8: Taking Charge of Your Journey

- Summarize the key concepts and teachings presented in the Introduction and Chapter 1 of this handbook.

- Reflect on your understanding of the Quantum Field and your identity as Energy-You. How has this knowledge impacted your perspective on life?

- Identify specific actions and choices you can make to manifest and engage with reality more intentionally.

- Consider the challenges you may encounter in your journey and how they can lead to growth and fulfillment.

- Express your commitment to making the most of your time on Earth and aligning with the energy of the Quantum Field for a more fulfilling life.

Final Thoughts: The Quantum Field's Message to You

The Quantum Field wants you to know that you are an integral part of it, experiencing life on this earthly plane as Energy-You. You have the authority to make choices and manifest reality as you desire. While life may present challenges, those challenges provide opportunities for growth and fulfillment.

The Quantum Field encourages you to embrace your true identity and live your life with intention, making the most of your time here. Remember that you are eternal and your consciousness will continue beyond this physical existence. By aligning with the energy of the Quantum Field, you can manifest fulfilling outcomes and create a life filled with love, joy, success, and fulfillment.

The journey ahead may have twists and turns, but with the wisdom and guidance of the Quantum Field, you have the power to influence your life and make it extraordinary. As you continue on your path, know that the Quantum Field is always with you, supporting your growth, success, and reunion. Your journey is the fulfillment and the possibilities are endless. Embrace the power within you and make the most of this precious gift called life.

Chapter Two

Study Guide for Chapter 2: What Your Self Is

Instructions: Use the information provided in Chapter 2 to answer the following questions and complete the activities. Consider your own beliefs and experiences as you work through each section. Feel free to take notes or reflect on your responses.

Section 1: Understanding Your Self and Its Collaborators

- Define, in your own words, the three collaborators of your self:

  - You (nonphysical energy):

  - Your body (and brain):

  - Your reality (other people, places, and things):

- Consider the interdependence of your self's collaborators. How does each collaborator contribute to the functioning of your self as a system? Provide examples for each collaborator.

- <u>Activity 1: Self-Reflection.</u> Take some time to reflect on the concept of your self being a system of three collaborators: You (nonphysical energy), your body (and brain), and your reality. Consider how each collaborator plays a role in your life and how they interact with one another.

- Questions

    - How do you currently perceive yourself and your role in life?

    - How do you make decisions in your daily life and what influences your choices?

    - Reflect on the interconnectedness of your three collaborators. How do they work together to create your reality?

- <u>Activity 2: Visualization Exercise.</u> Close your eyes and visualize yourself as the CEO of your own corporation, where the corporation represents your self. Imagine yourself making decisions, creating plans, and leading your self to success. Visualize your three collaborators working in harmony, supporting your vision, and manifesting your desires.

Section 2: Leadership of Your Self

- Imagine yourself as the CEO of your self. What responsibilities and decision-making authority do you have as the leader? List at least three.

- Explain why your role as the CEO of your self is crucial. How does your leadership impact the overall success and well-being of your self?

- Write about the qualities and actions that characterize effective leadership for your self. How can you make good decisions and follow through on them? Provide examples.

- Describe the importance of transparency and accountability in your leadership role. How can transparency foster trust and engagement with your collaborators? How does accountability contribute to your self's success?

- Activity 1: Leadership Vision Board. Create a vision board that represents your ideal self as a leader. Include images, words, and symbols that represent the qualities you want to embody as a CEO of your self. Display this vision board in a prominent place where you can see it daily.

  - Questions

    - What qualities do you believe are essential for effective leadership of your self?

    - How can you translate these qualities into actionable behaviors and decisions in your daily life?

- Activity 2: Decision-Making Exercise. Practice decision-making as the CEO of your self by setting small goals for the week. Write down the decisions you need to make to achieve these goals and follow through with them.

  - Questions:

    - How do you feel when you make decisions that align with your vision and goals?

    - What challenges do you encounter when trying to follow through on your decisions and how can you overcome them?

Section 3: The Power of Your Body and Brain

- Explain the significance of your body as a collaborator of your self. How can you lead your body effectively? Provide examples of actions and choices that promote optimal physical, emotional, and mental health.

- Write about the role of your brain in manifesting reality and engaging with it. How does your subconscious shape your reality? How does your conscious mind allow you to make choices and follow through on them?

- <u>Activity 1: Body-Mind Connection.</u> Engage in a physical activity that promotes the connection between your body and mind. Yoga, meditation, or mindful exercises can help you become more aware of your body and its signals.

  - Questions:

    - How does engaging in body-mind practices impact your overall well-being and decision-making abilities?

    - How can you prioritize self-care and physical health to better support your role as a leader?

- <u>Activity 2: Belief Inventory.</u> Take inventory of your beliefs about yourself, your abilities, and your reality. Write down both positive and limiting beliefs you may hold.

  - Questions:

    - How do your beliefs influence your reality and the choices you make?

    - Are there any limiting beliefs you want to change? Make note of them.

Section 4: Understanding Your Reality and Its Impact

- Explore the influence of your reality and the impact of others' versions of reality on your self. How can your manifestation and engagement with reality affect your success and well-being? How can others'?

- Write about the importance of feedback from your reality. How can your feelings serve as mirror-perfect feedback about the capability of your beliefs and the adequacy of your efforts? Provide examples.

- <u>Activity 1: Empathy Exercise.</u> Practice empathy by putting yourself in the shoes of someone whose reality is different from yours. Consider their beliefs, challenges, and aspirations.

    - Questions:

        - How can understanding and empathizing with others' realities improve your leadership abilities?

        - How can you foster connections and collaboration with others to create a more supportive and fulfilling reality for all?

- <u>Activity 2: Feedback Loop Reflection.</u> Reflect on the feedback your reality provides you through your feelings and experiences. Journal about the lessons you've learned from challenging situations and how they have influenced your growth.

    - Questions:

        - How can you use your emotions and experiences as valuable feedback to guide your decision-making and actions?

        - How can you respond to feedback and adjust your approach to improve your leadership of your self?

Section 5: Nurturing Your Self and Its Collaborators

- Activity 1: Self-Care Plan. Develop a self-care plan that includes activities to nurture each of your three collaborators: physical, mental, and emotional self-care.

  - Questions:

    - How can you integrate self-care practices into your daily routine to support your role as a leader?

    - What self-care activities align with your vision of yourself as a successful CEO of your self?

- Activity 2: Goal Setting for Growth. Set specific goals for personal growth and leadership development. Identify areas where you want to improve your decision-making, follow-through, or engagement with your reality.

  - Questions:

    - What specific leadership skills or qualities do you want to enhance, and how will you work on developing them?

    - How will achieving these goals positively impact your self and your ability to manifest a more fulfilling reality?

Section 6: Embracing Pain and Growth

- Reflect on the concept of embracing challenges and utilizing pain for personal growth. How can you learn from painful experiences and use them as catalysts for change and self-improvement?

- Write about the expectations and acceptance of both pleasure and pain in life. How can you navigate the inevitability of loss, pain, and displeasure while striving for the manifestation of your desires?

- Activity 1: Embracing Painful Feelings. When you encounter painful feelings, take the time to acknowledge and process them rather than suppressing or avoiding them. Journal about the insights gained from facing these emotions.

    - Questions:

        - How can embracing painful feelings help you better understand and address beliefs and areas that need growth?

        - How do you see pain as an opportunity for growth and learning rather than a hindrance?

- Activity 2: Cultivating Resilience. Practice resilience by setting realistic expectations for yourself and accepting that challenges are a natural part of life. Embrace setbacks as opportunities to learn and grow.

    - Questions:

        - How can cultivating resilience positively impact your leadership of your self and your ability to manifest your desires?

        - What strategies can you employ to bounce back from challenges and maintain focus on your vision?

Section 7: Integrating Leadership Into Your Life

- Activity 1: Daily Leadership Affirmations. Create a list of positive affirmations that reinforce your role as a capable leader of your self. Repeat these affirmations daily to reinforce your self-belief and confidence.

    - Questions:

        - How can affirmations help you stay focused on your vision and maintain a positive attitude in the face of challenges?

        - How do you see affirmations influencing your overall self-leadership and manifestation of reality?

- Activity 2: Impact on Others. Consider the impact of your self-leadership on others in your life. Reflect on how your choices and actions influence those around you.

    - Questions:

        - How does your self-leadership affect your relationships and interactions with others?

        - How can you use your self-leadership to inspire and support those you care about?

Section 8: Review and Continuing Growth

- Activity 1: Self-Study Journal. Maintain a self-study journal where you document your reflections, insights, and progress throughout this course. Review your entries regularly to track your growth.

- Questions:

    - How has this self-study course influenced your understanding of yourself, your self-leadership, and your manifestation of reality?

    - What specific lessons or insights do you want to carry forward as you continue to grow and develop as a leader of your self?

- Activity 2: Personal Manifestation Plan. Create a personal manifestation plan that outlines your long-term vision, goals, and action steps for the future. Use this plan to guide your ongoing self-leadership journey.

  - Questions:

    - How do you envision yourself leading your self in the future and what do you hope to achieve?

    - How will you continue to prioritize self-study, growth, and conscious manifestation of your reality going forward?

Conclusion

Congratulations on completing this self-study course on what your self is!

Reflect on the significance of leading your self effectively and embracing your role as the CEO. Consider the potential for growth, fulfillment, and success when you take charge of your actions, ideas, attitudes, and focus.

Through this guide, you have summarized key insights about your self and created actionable steps to enhance your leadership of your self. Well done!

This self-study course is a journey of personal exploration and growth. Embrace the process, be kind to yourself, and celebrate every step of your progress as you become the empowered CEO of your self. You have the power to shape your reality and create a more fulfilling life for yourself and others. Happy self-discovery and leadership!

Chapter Three

Study Guide for Chapter 3: How You Manifest and Engage With Your Reality

Instructions: Use the information provided in Chapter 3 to answer the following questions and complete the activities. Consider your own beliefs and experiences as you work through each section. Feel free to take notes or reflect on your responses.

Section 1: Understanding Consciousness and Reality

- What is the role of your brain in manifesting your reality?

- How does observation and awareness influence the manifestation of your reality?

- How do your beliefs shape your reality and the objects within it?

- <u>Activity 1: Reflection and Discussion.</u> Take some time to reflect on the concepts presented in the passage about consciousness and reality. Write down your thoughts and questions about the following points:

  - The relationship between consciousness and the brain as a quantum connection.

  - The role of beliefs in manifesting your unique version of life.

- The idea that material reality is made of energy and how this impacts your perception of the world.

Activity 2: Discussion. Discuss the reflections and questions from Activity 1 in a group setting or with at least one other person. Engage in an open conversation with others to gain different perspectives on these complex concepts. Listen to other's viewpoints and share your thoughts to enhance understanding.

Section 2: The Mechanics of Manifesting

- Describe the relationship between energy and material reality.

- Explain why material reality is considered temporary.

- What does it mean to say that an atom is mostly empty space?

- Activity 1: Creative Visualization. Create a vision board or draw a mind map representing your current beliefs and how they manifest in your reality. Use images, symbols, and colors to represent different aspects of your life that are influenced by your beliefs.

- Activity 2: Belief Analysis. Identify three beliefs that strongly influence your reality. Write them down and analyze their origins and impact on your life. Consider how these beliefs shape your actions, decisions, and engagement with the world. Reflect on whether these beliefs are serving you positively or negatively.

Section 3: How Real Is Your Reality?

- How does your consciousness contribute to manifesting your reality?

- Why is your version of reality unique to you?

- Reflect on a belief you have that has influenced the manifestation of your reality. How has it shaped your experiences?

- <u>Activity 1: Perception Experiment.</u> Choose an object in your environment and observe it closely, paying attention to its details. Then, close your eyes and visualize the object in your mind. Reflect on how your perception of the object changes when you observe it directly versus when you visualize it.

- <u>Activity 2: Understanding Energy.</u> Research different scientific concepts related to energy and its properties. Explore how energy is described in various fields such as physics, spirituality, and psychology. Write a short summary of your findings, discussing the implications of understanding energy in different contexts.

Section 4: An Atom Is Nothing

- <u>Activity 1: Atom Visualization.</u> Imagine an atom as described in the chapter – with a nucleus the size of a fruit fly in the center of a huge space like Yankee Stadium. Draw a simple diagram to create a visual representation of this concept.

- <u>Activity 2: Empty Space Reflection.</u> Reflect on the idea that 99.9999 percent of everything in your life is actually empty space or energy. Consider how this perspective can shift your perception of the physical world around you. Write a short essay exploring the implications of perceiving the world as mostly energy.

Section 5: Manifesting Is Making Nothing Into Something

- How does your conscious mind allow you to engage with reality?

- What role does your engagement play in shaping your experiences of reality?

- Share an example of a time when your engagement with reality made a significant impact on your experiences or outcomes.

- Activity 1: Mindful Manifestation. Choose a specific goal or desire you would like to manifest in your life. Practice mindfulness and visualization techniques to connect with the energy of your desire. Record your experiences and emotions during this process.

- Activity 2: Personal Manifestation Plan. Develop a step-by-step plan to manifest a specific goal or desire. Break down the process into actionable tasks and identify potential obstacles and limiting beliefs. Set a timeline for your manifestation plan and commit to taking consistent actions. Reflect on your progress regularly and make adjustments as needed.

Section 6: Manifesting Your Reality With Your Subconscious Mind

- What are the three access points where you can change your default settings?

- Activity 1: Subconscious Exploration. Engage in a meditation or visualization exercise to connect with your subconscious mind. Explore the beliefs and memories that shape your current reality. Take notes on any insights or revelations that arise during this process.

- Activity 2: Challenging Limiting Beliefs. Identify one or more limiting beliefs that you inherited during childhood and are still affecting your reality. Challenge these beliefs by examining evidence that contradicts them and finding alternative perspectives. Write a self-affirming statement that counteracts each limiting belief and practice repeating these affirmations regularly.

Section 7: Your Beliefs' Perfect Storage Place

- Share one belief you inherited that you would like to replace or modify. How can you actively work on changing this belief to manifest a different reality?

- Activity 1: Emotion-Focused Communication. Practice communicating with others using emotions rather than words. Share experiences, stories, or ideas with emotional expressions and observe how the emotions convey the essence of your message.

- Activity 2: Emotion Regulation Techniques. Explore different emotion regulation techniques such as mindfulness, deep breathing, and meditation. Experiment with these techniques and record their impact on your emotional state. Identify which techniques resonate with you the most.

Section 8: Manifesting Your Reality With Your Subconscious Mind

- Reflect on an area of your life where you would like to make changes. How can you apply intentional engagement techniques to shift your default settings in that area?

- Explain the concept of default manifesting and its impact on your life.

- How does default engagement affect your experiences of reality?

- Have you experienced any indicators that your default manifesting or engagement settings are not serving you? If yes, provide examples.

- Activity 1: Daily Conscious Engagement. For a week, keep a journal documenting your conscious engagement with reality. Write down your daily actions, decisions, and focus, as well as the outcomes of these engagements. Reflect on the impact of your conscious choices on your experiences and feelings.

- Activity 2: Intentional Engagement. Choose one area of your life where you want to make intentional changes in your engagement. Develop a plan to consciously shift your actions, attitudes, or focus in this area. Monitor your progress and journal about the effects of intentional engagement on your reality.

Conclusion

Congratulations on completing this self-study course on how you manifest and engage with your reality!

You have delved into profound concepts of consciousness, reality, manifesting, and engagement. Through a variety of activities you've gained a deeper understanding of yourself, your beliefs, and your power to shape your reality intentionally. You have been encouraged toward self-reflection and exploration, fostering a journey of personal growth and transformation. Learning is a lifelong process and each individual's experience will be unique as they embark on the path of self-discovery and self-empowerment.

Manifesting and engaging with reality is an ongoing process. Use your answers to this guide as a tool to continue exploring and refining your beliefs, actions, and choices as you work towards manifesting a more fulfilling and intentional life.

Chapter Four

Study Guide for Chapter 5: How to Intentionally Manifest Your Reality

Instructions:

- Carefully read the information provided in Chapter 5 about the belief-raising process.

- Reflect on your own life as you use this part of the guide.

- Complete each part of the belief-raising process, as outlined below.

- Engage in the different types of questions and activities to enhance your learning experience.

Section One: Introduction to Intentional Manifesting

- <u>Activity 1: Reflecting on Your Beliefs.</u> Take a moment to reflect on your current beliefs about manifesting and how they may be influencing your reality. Write down any thoughts, beliefs, or doubts you have about your ability to intentionally manifest what you desire.

- <u>Activity 2: Setting Intentions.</u> Think about a specific area of your life where you would like to see positive changes. It could be related to relationships, career, health, or personal growth. Set an intention for what you want to manifest in this area and write it down as a clear and positive statement.

Section Two: Understanding Your Emotional Perspective

- <u>Activity 1: Identifying Painful Feelings.</u> Choose the area of your life that you want to work on manifesting. Write about the painful feelings you associate with this area. Be completely honest with yourself and let your emotions flow onto the page without judgment.

  - Choose a Painful Part of Your Reality:

    - Write down the specific desire that is painfully absent from your life.

  - Get To Your True Feelings by Writing about Them:

    - Answer the following questions about the absence of your desire:

      - How do I really feel about the absence of this desire?

      - How do I feel about me, my worth, my value, and what others think?

  - Write down all the unpleasant feelings that come up when you declare your desire aloud.

  - Be Radically Self-Honest:

    - Write about your painful thoughts and feelings without analyzing or judging them.

- Keep in mind that this writing is private and for your personal growth.

- Activity 2: Recognizing Emotional Patterns. Use the Emotional Reference Chart provided in Chapter 4 of the book to identify your current emotional perspective about the chosen area of your life. Take note of where you are on the chart and reflect on how your emotions are influencing your reality in this particular area.

  - Find Your Starting Point on the Emotional Reference Chart:

    - Use the Emotional Reference Chart provided in the book to identify the emotional perspective that matches your current feelings.

    - Choose the emotional perspective that aligns best with your writing.

    - Take note of where you are on the chart and reflect on how your emotions are influencing your reality in this particular area.

Section Three: Moving Toward Alignment

- Activity 1: Setting a New Target Emotional Perspective. Based on the Emotional Reference Chart, select the next highest emotional perspective from your current position. This will be your new target emotional perspective. Write about how you would feel and perceive your chosen area of life from this new perspective.

  - Write about Your Absent Desire from This New Target Perspective:

    - Write down the names of the new target emotions.

    - Look up the definitions of the new emotions.

- Answer the following questions based on the new emotions:

  - What must I believe about myself and my life to feel this way about not having my desire?

  - How would this part of reality need to work for me to feel this way?

  - What would it mean about my worth, value, and what others think of me to feel this way?

- Use the definitions of the new target emotions as prompts to guide your writing. Be radically self-honest and write in free-form.

- Activity 2: Embracing Incremental Growth. Manifest your chosen area of life from your new target emotional perspective. Envision yourself living from this perspective and notice any changes in your thoughts, actions, or feelings. Embrace the incremental growth and small improvements as they come.

- Activity 3: Manifest It. To the best of your ability, manifest this area of your life from your new perspective.

  - See and understand your chosen desire from the perspective of the new emotional perspective.

  - Imagine yourself as an actor playing a role with the new script you've written.

  - Consider how you would act and how that would change the whole production.

Section Four: Overcoming Resistance

- Activity 1: Dealing with Resistance. Reflect on any resistance you may be experiencing while trying to manifest from a new emotional perspective. Write down any fears, doubts, or limiting beliefs that might be holding you back.

- Activity 2: Reassuring Your Subconscious. Craft affirmations and statements that reassure your subconscious that the changes you're making are safe and aligned with your growth. Repeat these affirmations regularly to reinforce positive beliefs.

  - Reassure Your Subconscious:

    - Acknowledge any hesitancy you may feel about manifesting from the new perspective.

    - Assure your subconscious that the new perspective is safe and believable.

Section Five: Embracing Patience and Persistence

- Activity 1: Cultivating Patience. Acknowledge that the belief-raising process is gradual and requires patience. Write about how you can stay patient and trust the journey, even when progress seems slow.

  - The Slight Improvements Will Get You There:

    - Understand that each improvement, no matter how small, is significant.

    - Embrace incremental growth and change.

- Activity 2: Celebrating Progress. Celebrate each incremental improvement and shift towards alignment. Note your progress and the positive changes you observe in your life in your belief-raising writing.

Section Six: The Journey to the Top

- Activity 1: Embracing the Journey. Reflect on the changes you've already witnessed in your chosen area of life and how they align with your new emotional perspective. Embrace the growth and transformation that has taken place within you as you continue writing and living your way to the top of the Chart.

  - Continuously work your way up the Emotional Reference Chart.

  - Repeat the writing and living cycle each day until you reach "Love and Ecstasy" on the Emotional Reference Chart.

- Activity 2: Envisioning Your Future Reality. While allowing yourself to imagine yourself at the top of the Emotional Reference Chart, manifesting from a state of love and ecstasy, continue to write about how your life looks and feels from your current emotional perspective. Stick to the pace of writing and living your way one emotional perspective higher at a time.

Section 7: Implementing Belief-Raising in Other Areas

- Activity 1: Identifying New Areas for Growth. Take time to identify other areas of your life that may benefit from the belief-raising process. Choose one specific desire to focus on next and set your intention for growth in that area.

- Activity 2: Repeating the Process. Repeat the belief-raising process for your new area of focus. Embrace the incremental growth and apply the same dedication and honesty to your writing and manifesting practice.

Section 8: Reflecting on Your Journey

- Activity 1: Self-Reflection. Reflect on your belief-raising journey and the changes you've witnessed in various areas of your life. Write about any lessons you've learned and how your perception of manifesting has evolved.

- Activity 2: Gratitude and Ongoing Growth. Express gratitude for the growth and transformation you've experienced. Commit to ongoing self-awareness and using intentional manifesting to align your beliefs with your desires throughout your life journey.

Conclusion

Congratulations on completing this self-study course on intentional manifesting and belief-raising!

- Celebrate your progress and commitment to radical self-honesty.

- Embrace the opportunities for growth and change that this process provides.

- Keep persisting and discovering new ways to manifest your desires differently.

You now have the tools and understanding to create positive changes in your life by aligning your beliefs with your desires. Remember that manifesting is an ongoing journey of growth and self-awareness. Embrace each step of the process, be patient with yourself, and continue to manifest from a place of love, empowerment, and alignment. Happy manifesting!

<u>Note:</u> Remember to keep your writing private and create a safe space for yourself to explore your emotions and thoughts without judgment.

Chapter Five

Study Guide for Chapter 6: How to Intentionally Engage with Your Reality

Instructions:

- Read the information provided on vibrational alignment and maximizing opportunities in Chapter 6 of the book.

- Engage with the activities and questions designed to help you align yourself with the opportunities in each moment.

- Reflect on your responses and use them as a guide to start your day in vibrational alignment.

Section 1: Introduction to Vibrational Alignment

- Reflect on the importance of daily vibrational alignment, even on days when you don't feel naturally excited.

    - Write about why it is essential to align yourself with opportunities, regardless of circumstances or emotions.

    - Describe how you can make a commitment to vibrational alignment and prioritize it in your daily routine.

- Consider the potential benefits and outcomes of consistent alignment with opportunities.

- Activity 1: Reflective Journaling. Take a moment to journal about your understanding of vibrational alignment and its importance in engaging with reality. Write about any experiences you've had where aligning yourself with opportunities made a difference in your performance or outcomes.

- Activity 2: Mindful Breathing and Affirmation Practice. Sit in a comfortable position and focus on your breath, taking slow, deep breaths in and out. While you breathe, repeat an affirmation related to your vibrational alignment. For example, "I am capable of being aligned with the opportunities presented to me in each moment today." Synchronize your breath with the affirmation, inhaling positivity and exhaling any tension or negative energy.

Section 2: Morning Journaling for Vibrational Alignment

- Activity 1: Visual Representation. Create a visual representation of your vibrational alignment process. This could be in the form of a mind map, flowchart, or a series of illustrations that depict how you prepare yourself to engage with reality each morning.

- Activity 2: Daily Journaling Practice. Begin each morning by journaling in free form about the opportunities that await you in the day ahead. Let your thoughts and feelings flow onto the page without editing or censoring yourself.
    - Reflect on the preciousness of each moment:
        - How does it feel to know that each moment is an opportunity to engage with reality?

- Write about the value of being fully present and alive in this moment.

Section 3: Aligning with Opportunities, Not Outcomes

- Aligning with your opportunities:

  - What opportunities do you see in the day ahead? List them and describe their significance.

  - How can you align yourself with these opportunities to give your best effort in each moment?

- Activity 1: Opportunity vs. Outcome Analysis. Reflect on past experiences where you were more focused on the outcomes rather than the opportunities themselves. What were the consequences of this approach? Contrast it with times when you aligned yourself with opportunities, regardless of the outcome.

- Activity 2: Opportunities Mindset Poster. Design a motivational poster that reminds you to focus on aligning with opportunities, not outcomes. Include quotes, images, and symbols that inspire you to stay present and engaged with each moment.

Section 4: Aligning Under Any Circumstances

- Activity 1: Emotional Intelligence Practice. Develop your emotional intelligence by identifying and acknowledging your emotions, even in challenging circumstances. Practice journaling about how you can align yourself with opportunities despite not feeling positive or upbeat.

- Activity 2: Personal Affirmations. Create a list of personal affirmations that remind you of your strengths, capabilities, and resilience. Use these affirmations to reinforce your ability to align with opportunities, no matter how you feel.

Section 5: Taking Control of What's in Your Control

- Acknowledging your control:

    - Reflect on the things you have control over in your life.

    - How can you take charge of these aspects to maximize your engagement with reality?

- Activity 1: Circle of Influence Exercise. Draw a circle and divide it into two sections: "Things in My Control" and "Things Not in My Control." List aspects of your life in each section. Reflect on how focusing on what you can control enhances your ability to align with opportunities.

- Activity 2: Personal Action Plan. Create a personal action plan that outlines specific steps you can take to control the factors that influence your ability to be prepared and engaged with reality.

Section 6: Correlation and Communication

- Reflect on the concept of correlation and how it relates to aligning with opportunities.

    - Choose a person, place, or thing in your life that you would like to correlate with. Write about how you can communicate and correlate with this aspect of your reality to maximize opportunities.

- Consider how aligning yourself with this correlation can enhance your engagement with reality.

- Activity 1: Visualization Exercise. Practice a visualization exercise where you mentally communicate with your future self about taking advantage of opportunities. Imagine yourself successfully aligning with opportunities and the positive outcomes that result.

- Activity 2: Guided Meditation. Engage in a meditation session focused on correlating with each moment and the opportunities it presents. Use this meditation as a daily practice to enhance your vibrational alignment.

Section 7: Alignment on Challenging Days

- Recall a time when you felt discouraged or had negative thoughts about your life or abilities.

  - Write about that experience, acknowledging your feelings and thoughts.

  - Challenge those negative thoughts by identifying the positive aspects and potential opportunities.

  - Describe how you can align yourself with opportunities, despite negative emotions or circumstances.

- Activity 1: Gratitude Journaling. Keep a gratitude journal and write down three things you are grateful for each day. Reflect on how practicing gratitude helps you align with opportunities even on challenging days.

- Activity 2: Inspirational Quotes Collection. Compile a collection of inspirational quotes that resonate with you and lift your spirits on difficult days. Use these quotes to motivate yourself to align with opportunities despite external circumstances.

Section 8: Making Vibrational Alignment a Habit

- Activity 1: Habit Tracker. Create a habit tracker to monitor your daily morning journaling and alignment practice. Use visual cues or symbols to mark each day you successfully complete the practice.

- Activity 2: Self-Assessment and Progress Report. Conduct a self-assessment to evaluate your progress in developing vibrational alignment with opportunities. Set new goals and intentions based on your experiences using this guide.

Conclusion

Congratulations on completing this self-study course on intentional engagement and vibrational alignment with opportunities!

Engaging with reality in a deliberate and aligned manner is an ongoing practice. Continue to journal, meditate, and align yourself with opportunities to manifest your best performances and create the reality you desire. By understanding and applying these principles, you can experience greater fulfillment and success in all aspects of your life. Keep learning, growing, and aligning with the endless possibilities that each moment offers!

Take a few moments to reflect on your responses and the insights gained from completing these questions and activities. Consider how you can apply the principles of vibrational alignment and maximizing opportunities in your daily life.

Commit to starting each day in vibrational alignment and embrace the potential for growth, success, and fulfillment in each moment.

Chapter Six

Study Guide for Chapter 7, Technique 1: Give Your Best Effort to Follow Form

Instructions: Use the information provided in Chapter 7, Technique 1 to answer the following questions and complete the activities. Consider your own beliefs and experiences as you work through each section. Feel free to take notes or reflect on your responses.

Section 1: Introduction to Following Form

- Reflect on the concept of giving your best effort to follow form in different areas of your life. How does the idea of aligning your actions, ideas, attitudes, and focus with a blueprint resonate with you? Write down your thoughts and initial insights.

- <u>Activity 1: Reflective Journaling.</u> Take some time to journal about your understanding of "following form" and its potential impact on your life. Reflect on experiences where you followed a specific blueprint or form and how it affected your outcomes and performance.

- Activity 2: Learner Choice. Choose one or more of the following activities to further explore the concept of following form:

  - Visual learner: Create a visual representation (e.g., a poster, infographic) that illustrates the elements and benefits of following form in personal growth and success.

  - Auditory learner: Record yourself explaining the concept of following form and its significance in your own words. Listen to it for reinforcement and reflection.

  - Kinesthetic learner: Engage in a physical activity (e.g., yoga, dance) that allows you to embody the idea of following form. Reflect on your experience afterward.

Section 2: Identifying the Right Form

- Choose an important aspect of your life that you want to improve or be more successful in.

- Activity 1: Role Model Research. Identify a person who has successfully manifested a specific aspect of life you want to improve or achieve. This person should serve as your role model for "following form." Research their success habits, practices, and mindset through books, podcasts, or online resources.

  - Chosen Aspect:

  - Person/Resource:

- Activity 2: Form Blueprint. Create a "form blueprint" that outlines the specific habits, actions, attitudes, and focus of your chosen role model. Dive deep into understanding their form by studying the success habits, best practices, and mindset of the person or resource you chose. Take notes on their approach, strategies, and insights. Use visual aids, such as charts or diagrams, to make the blueprint easily digestible.

  - Key Elements of the Form:

Section 3: Adopting the Form

- Activity 1: Daily Form Emulation. Dedicate at least 150 minutes per week (approximately 20 minutes a day) to actively following the learned form in the chosen aspect of your life. Practice the success habits, incorporate the best practices, and adopt the recommended mindset.

  - Weekly Time Commitment:

- Activity 2: Reflection and Self-Assessment. Regularly reflect on your efforts to follow this form. Assess how well you are incorporating the habits and practices into your daily life. Identify areas where you excel and where improvement is needed.

- Activity 3: Learner Choice. Choose one of more of the following activities to further explore the concept of following form:

  - Visual learner: Create a flowchart or diagram that outlines the steps and components of giving your best effort to follow form.

  - Auditory learner: Record affirmations or statements that align with the mindset and actions required to follow form. Listen to them regularly.

- Kinesthetic learner: Engage in the chosen aspect of your life with a heightened awareness of following form. Practice the recommended success habits and reflect on your experience afterward.

Section 4: Understanding the Benefits

- Reflect on the four distinct ways that giving your best effort to follow form helps your performance, as described in the book How do these benefits resonate with your understanding of personal growth and success? Write down your thoughts and insights.

- Choose one benefit from the list (assigning jobs to your whole self, illuminating where help is needed, providing an internal litmus test, taking pressure off) and explore it further. Discuss how it manifests in your own experiences of following form and the impact it has on your overall well-being and performance.

- <u>Activity 1: Personal Success Stories.</u> Write a personal success story or anecdote about a time when following form positively impacted your performance or outcomes. Share this story with a friend, family member, or in an online community for feedback and encouragement.

- <u>Activity 2: Visualization Exercise.</u> Engage in a visualization exercise where you imagine yourself successfully following form and achieving your desired outcomes. Visualize how this success positively impacts your life and well-being.

Section 5: Dealing with Challenges and Setbacks

- Consider real-life situations where you can apply the concept of giving your best effort to follow form. Choose specific aspects or challenges in your life that could benefit from this approach.

  - Situation 1:

  - Situation 2:

  - Situation 3:

- Write a detailed action plan for each situation, outlining the steps you will take to give your best effort to follow form. Include specific actions, ideas, attitudes, and focus that align with the form you want to emulate.

  - Action Plan for Situation 1:

  - Action Plan for Situation 2:

  - Action Plan for Situation 3:

- <u>Activity 1: Resilience Building.</u> Develop resilience by identifying and addressing potential challenges and setbacks that may arise when following form. Create a plan to overcome these obstacles and maintain your commitment to giving your best effort.

- <u>Activity 2: Failure as a Learning Opportunity.</u> Reframe the concept of failure as a learning opportunity rather than a personal flaw. Write about a time when you faced setbacks while following form and how you used the experience to grow and improve.

Section 6: Cultivating Self-Compassion

- Reflect on the significance of giving your best effort to follow form in the areas of your life that matter most to you. How does this knowledge impact your perspective on personal growth, success, and engagement with reality? Write down your thoughts and insights.

- Activity 1: Self-Compassion Journaling. Engage in self-compassion journaling to foster a sense of kindness and understanding towards yourself. Write about your efforts to follow form, acknowledging that it's okay to make mistakes and that progress is more important than perfection.

- Activity 2: Self-Compassion Visualization. Practice a guided visualization exercise focused on self-compassion. Imagine yourself offering kindness and encouragement to your past, present, and future self as you navigate the journey of following form.

Section 7: Tracking Progress and Celebrating Success

- Consider future scenarios where you can actively give your best effort to follow form in different aspects of your life. Write down potential situations and moments where you can embody the concept of following form for personal growth and success.

- Activity 1: Progress Tracker. Create a progress tracker to monitor your daily efforts to follow form. Use this tracker to record your successes and challenges, and identify patterns that may influence your progress.

- Activity 2: Celebration Ritual. Design a celebration ritual to mark milestones and achievements in your journey of following form. Celebrate your dedication and growth, regardless of the specific outcomes you've achieved.

Section 8: Making Following Form a Way of Life

- Reflect on the insights gained from exploring the concept of giving your best effort to follow form and applying it to real-life situations. How do you feel about the potential for personal growth and success through following form? Write a brief paragraph summarizing your thoughts and any further actions you plan to take to fully embrace this approach.

- Write a personal commitment statement outlining your dedication to incorporating giving your best effort to follow form into your regular practice. Include specific aspects, situations, and intentions for personal growth and success.

- <u>Activity: Form Integration Plan.</u> Develop a plan to integrate the lessons and habits of following form into various aspects of your life. Identify areas beyond your initial focus where following form can bring positive changes.

Conclusion

Congratulations on completing this self-study course on giving your best effort to follow form!

This practice is an ongoing journey of growth and self-improvement. Continue to adopt the habits and practices of successful role models and be compassionate towards yourself as you navigate challenges and setbacks. By embracing the concept of following form and dedicating your best effort to it, you are enhancing your ability to manifest your desires and engage with reality on a more fulfilling level. Keep learning, adapting, and following form to create the life you truly desire!

Chapter Seven

Study Guide for Chapter 7, Technique 2: Satisfy Your Critic

Instructions: Use the information provided in Chapter 7, Technique 2 to answer the following questions and complete the activities. Consider your own beliefs and experiences as you work through each section. Feel free to take notes or reflect on your responses.

Section 1: Introduction to Satisfying Your Critic

- Activity 1: Self-Reflection. Take some time to reflect on past experiences when you received criticism, both from external sources and self-criticism. How did you react to it? Did you find it helpful or demotivating? Consider how satisfying your critic could have positively impacted your performance and outcomes.

- Activity 2: Learner Choice. Choose one or more of the following activities to further explore the concept of satisfying your critic:

  - Visual learner: Create a visual representation (e.g., a mind map, infographic) that depicts the process of satisfying your critic and its impact on personal growth.

- Auditory learner: Record yourself explaining the concept of satisfying your critic and its benefits. Listen to it for reinforcement and reflection.

- Kinesthetic learner: Engage in a physical activity (e.g., role-playing, journaling) that simulates a conversation with your critic. Reflect on the experience and identify key insights.

Section 2: Understanding the Concept of Satisfying Your Critic

- Consider the concept of satisfying your critic and its significance in personal growth and success. How does the idea of addressing criticism, both internal and external, resonate with you? Write down your thoughts and initial insights.

- Activity 1: Define Your Terms. Create your own definition of "satisfying your critic" based on the information from the book. Explain the benefits and potential challenges associated with this technique.

- Activity 2: Case Study Analysis. Read or watch a case study of someone who successfully satisfied their critics, either from external sources or internal self-criticism. Analyze their experiences, identifying the strategies they used and the outcomes they achieved.

Section 3: Identifying Your Critics

- Activity 1: Critic Inventory. Create a list of the people or sources that have criticized you or your performance in different areas of your life. Categorize each critic as either constructive or potentially a hater.

- Activity 2: Self-Criticism Reflection. Engage in reflective journaling about instances of self-criticism. Identify recurring patterns or themes and consider how you can differentiate between constructive self-criticism and self-hating thoughts.

Section 4: The Process of Satisfying Your Critic

- Review the steps outlined in the book on how to satisfy your critic. Write down the steps in your own words to ensure you have a clear understanding.

- Choose a specific situation in your life where you have faced criticism or self-criticism. Describe the situation and the nature of the criticism you received or imposed on yourself.

  - Chosen Situation:

  - Nature of Criticism:

- Activity 1: Understanding Expectations. Practice active listening and communication skills when receiving criticism. Learn how to identify the specific expectations of your critics without becoming defensive or argumentative.

- Activity 2: Creating an Action Plan. Develop an action plan for addressing the criticisms you've received. Break down each expectation and outline the steps you will take to satisfy your critics in various aspects of your life.

  - Step 1: Seek a clear understanding of the criticism from your critic's perspective without defending yourself. Reflect on your mindset and approach during this process.

  - Step 2: Identify how you can meet your critic's expectations in a reasonable, appropriate, legal, moral, and ethical manner. Develop a plan or strategy to address the issue.

- Step 3: Communicate your intentions to your critic and a trustworthy third party, sharing the expectations you will satisfy and how you will do so. Consider the importance of transparency and accountability.

- Step 4: Follow through on your plan and strive to meet your critic's expectations. Reflect on the effort and improvements you make in addressing the criticism.

Section 5: Overcoming Challenges and Internal Obstacles

- Consider real-life situations where you can apply the concept of satisfying your critic. Choose specific aspects or challenges in your life where addressing criticism is necessary for personal growth.

  - Situation 1:

  - Situation 2:

  - Situation 3:

- Write a detailed action plan for each situation, outlining the steps you will take to satisfy your critic and address the criticism constructively. Include specific actions, strategies, and mindset shifts that align with the concept of satisfying your critic.

  - Action Plan for Situation 1:

  - Action Plan for Situation 2:

- Action Plan for Situation 3:

- Activity 1: Overcoming Resistance. Identify any resistance you may have to satisfying your critics. Are there any mental or emotional barriers preventing you from addressing criticism constructively? Develop strategies to overcome these obstacles.

- Activity 2: Visualization Exercise. Engage in a guided visualization exercise where you imagine yourself confidently addressing criticism and successfully satisfying your critics. Visualize the positive outcomes of this process in different areas of your life.

Section 6: Building Transparent Accountability

- Reflect on the significance of satisfying your critic in your life and its potential to enhance personal growth and success. How does this knowledge impact your perspective on handling criticism and striving for improvement? Write down your thoughts and insights.

- Activity 1: Accountability Partner. Find a trustworthy accountability partner, such as a friend or family member, to support you in your journey of satisfying your critics. Share your action plan with them and discuss ways they can help hold you accountable.

- Activity 2: Progress Check-ins. Regularly check-in with your accountability partner to share your progress in meeting the expectations of your critics. Discuss any challenges you've faced and celebrate your successes along the way.

Section 7: Embracing Feedback for Growth

- Reflect on the four distinct ways that satisfying your critic helps your personal growth and performance, as described in the text. How do these benefits resonate with your understanding of addressing criticism and pursuing success? Write down your thoughts and insights.

- Choose one benefit from the list (separates haters from allies, productively employs almost anyone, reveals blind spots, works with any critic) and explore it further. Discuss how it manifests in your own experiences of satisfying your critic and the impact it has on your personal growth and relationships.

- <u>Activity 1: Feedback Loop.</u> Develop a feedback loop system where you actively seek feedback from your critics after implementing changes to satisfy their expectations. Use this feedback to refine your approach and continuously improve.

- <u>Activity 2: Growth Mindset Journaling.</u> Engage in growth mindset journaling, focusing on the lessons and growth opportunities presented by criticism. Write about how satisfying your critics has contributed to your personal and professional development.

Section 8: Integrating Satisfying Your Critic as a Habit

- Consider future scenarios where you can actively satisfy your critic in different aspects of your life. Write down potential situations and moments where addressing criticism constructively can lead to personal growth and improved performance.

- Write a personal commitment statement outlining your dedication to incorporating satisfying your critic into your regular practice. Include specific aspects, situations, and intentions for embracing criticism as an opportunity for growth.

- Activity 1: Long-Term Goal Setting. Set long-term goals for how you will continue to use the technique of satisfying your critic in different areas of your life. Outline your vision for personal and professional growth and how this process will support it.

- Activity 2: Final Reflection. Conduct a final reflection on your self-study journey. Write about the insights you've gained, the challenges you've overcome, and how satisfying your critic has positively impacted your performance and engagement with reality.

Conclusion

Congratulations on completing this self-study course on satisfying your critic!

Remember that this process is not about seeking external validation or approval but rather about using criticism constructively to improve your performance and achieve your goals. By addressing feedback from both external sources and self-criticism, you are gaini valuable insights into blind spots and opportunities for growth.

Embrace the feedback loop and continue to build transparent accountability to foster continuous improvement in all areas of your life. With this powerful technique, you can confidently navigate criticism, develop resilience, and manifest a more fulfilling reality. Keep practicing and integrating the concept of satisfying your critic as a habit to achieve long-term success and personal development.

Chapter Eight

Study Guide for Chapter 7, Technique 3: Use Your Board of Directors

Instructions: Use the information provided in Chapter 7, Technique 3 to answer the following questions and complete the activities. Consider your own beliefs and experiences as you work through each section. Feel free to take notes or reflect on your responses.

Section 1: Introduction to Using Your Board of Directors

- <u>Activity: Self-Reflection.</u> Reflect on the areas of your life where you seek to manifest and engage with your desires. Consider the challenges you've faced in these areas and how having a board of directors could have helped you overcome them.

- <u>Activity 2: Learner Choice.</u> Choose one or more of the following activities to further explore the concept of using a board of directors:

  - Visual learner: Create a visual representation (e.g., a mind map, diagram) that illustrates the concept of using a board of directors and its impact on manifestation and growth.

  - Auditory learner: Record yourself explaining the manifesting concept of forming and using your board of directors. Listen for reinforcement and reflection.

- Kinesthetic learner: Engage in a role-playing activity where you act out a meeting with your board of directors, practicing how to communicate and seek advice. Reflect on the experience and identify key insights.

Section 2: Understanding the Concept of Using Your Board of Directors

- Reflect on the concept of using a board of directors in your personal life and its significance in manifestation and growth. How does the idea of gathering trustworthy and qualified advisors resonate with you? Write down your thoughts and initial insights.

- <u>Activity 1: Define Your Terms.</u> Create your own definition of "using your board of directors" based on the provided information. Explain the benefits and potential challenges associated with this technique.

- <u>Activity 2: Case Study Analysis.</u> Read or watch a case study of someone who has successfully used their board of directors to achieve their goals. Analyze their experiences, identifying the strategies they used and the outcomes they achieved.

Section 3: Identifying Your Board Members

- Review the steps outlined in the book on how to use your board of directors. Write down the steps in your own words to ensure you have a clear understanding.

- Choose a specific aspect of your life where you want to manifest and engage with the most important parts as you desire. Describe the aspect and the emotions associated with it.

    - Chosen Aspect:

    - Emotions Associated:

- Identify three to four individuals in your life who possess the highest levels of trustworthiness, investment in you, and expertise related to the chosen aspect. These individuals should be willing to actively support and advise you in achieving your goals. Write down their names and a brief description of their qualifications.

    - Board Member 1:

    - Board Member 2:

    - Board Member 3:

    - Board Member 4 (optional):

- <u>Activity 1: Board Member Inventory.</u> Write a paragraph introducing each potential board member, considering people you have personal access to who possess high levels of trustworthiness, investment in you, and expertise in the areas you're focusing on.

- <u>Activity 2: Formal Invitation.</u> Develop a formal invitation template that you can use to ask potential board members if they are willing to be a part of your board of directors. Consider the key points you want to communicate to them.

Section 4: Establishing a Transparent Board Relationship

- Practice the steps of using your board of directors in relation to the chosen aspect of your life. Perform the following actions:

  - Step 1: Formally ask each identified individual if they are willing to be a part of your board of directors and meet with you regularly to provide guidance and support. If someone declines, accept it as a sign that it may not be the right match at this time.

  - Step 2: Once you have received buy-in from your board members, schedule regular meetings with each of them. Aim to meet at least once a month, either in person or via phone/video call.

  - Step 3: Share relevant information and updates with your board members between meetings to keep them informed and engaged. This can include progress reports, challenges faced, and goals for the upcoming period.

  - Step 4: During your meetings, be transparent about your efforts, follow-through, and results related to the chosen aspect. Seek advice, listen attentively, and be accountable to your board members for delivering on your goals.

- Activity 1: The First Meeting. Plan a mock first meeting with a potential board member. Practice introducing the concept of your board of directors, explaining your goals, and seeking their commitment to the process.

- Activity 2: Communication Strategies. Explore different communication tools and techniques that will help you maintain transparency with your board members between meetings. Consider using email updates, shared documents, or video calls.

Section 5: Leveraging Your Board's Expertise

- Consider real-life situations where you can apply the concept of using a board of directors. Choose specific aspects or goals in your life where seeking guidance and accountability from qualified advisors can lead to improved manifestation and personal growth.

    - Situation/Goal 1:

    - Situation/Goal 2:

    - Situation/Goal 3:

- Write a detailed action plan for each situation, outlining how you will actively involve your board of directors to support your manifestation and personal growth. Include specific actions, strategies, and communication methods that align with utilizing your board of directors.

    - Action Plan for Situation/Goal 1:

    - Action Plan for Situation/Goal 2:

    - Action Plan for Situation/Goal 3:

- <u>Activity 1: Forming Subgroups.</u> Divide your board members into subgroups based on their expertise in specific areas of your goals. Create a plan for meeting with these subgroups individually to gather targeted feedback.

- <u>Activity 2: Board Member Collaboration.</u> Encourage collaboration between your board members. Facilitate discussions or brainstorming sessions where they can share insights and ideas to support your progress.

Section 6: Embracing Accountability and Growth

- Reflect on the significance of using a board of directors in your life and its potential to enhance manifestation and personal growth. How does this knowledge impact your perspective on seeking guidance and accountability? Write down your thoughts and insights.

- Reflect on the four distinct ways that using your board of directors helps in manifestation and growth, as described in the text. How do these benefits resonate with your understanding of seeking guidance and accountability? Write down your thoughts and insights.

- Choose one benefit from the list (getting the right people in the right seats on the bus, directing attention to those whose opinions matter most, utilizing the power of two, allowing advisors to grow with you) and explore it further. Discuss how it manifests in your own experiences of using a board of directors and the impact it has on your manifestation and personal growth.

- Activity 1: Board Member Feedback. Practice receiving feedback from your board members with an open mind and without becoming defensive. Develop strategies to implement their suggestions and improve your form and effort.

- Activity 2: Reflective Journaling. Engage in reflective journaling after each board meeting, writing about the key insights gained, action items identified, and your emotional response to the feedback received.

Section 7: Adapting and Expanding Your Board

- Reflect on the insights gained from exploring the concept of using a board of directors and applying it to real-life situations. How do you feel about the potential for enhancing your manifestation and personal growth through this approach? Write a brief paragraph summarizing your thoughts and any further actions you plan to take to fully embrace this concept.

- Activity 1: Growth and Change Assessment. Regularly assess your goals and progress to identify areas where you may need new or additional board members. Consider the qualifications and expertise needed for each position.

- Activity 2: Inviting New Members. Create a plan for inviting new board members to join your board of directors. Consider how you will approach potential candidates and explain the value of their involvement.

Section 8: Integrating the Board of Directors Approach

- Consider future scenarios where you can actively use your board of directors in different aspects of your life. Write down potential situations and moments where seeking guidance and accountability from qualified advisors can support your manifestation and personal growth.

- Write a personal commitment statement outlining your dedication to involving your board of directors in your regular practice. Include specific aspects, situations, and intentions for seeking guidance and utilizing accountability to enhance your manifestation and personal growth.

- Activity 1: Long-Term Goal Setting. Set long-term goals for how you will continue to use your board of directors to support your personal and professional growth. Outline your vision for leveraging their guidance in the future.

- Activity 2: Final Reflection. Conduct a final reflection on your self-study journey of using your board of directors. Write about the insights you've gained, the challenges you've overcome, and how this approach has positively impacted your ability to manifest and engage with your desires.

Conclusion

Congratulations on completing this self-study course on using your board of directors!

You have learned a powerful technique to enhance your personal and professional growth by leveraging the expertise and guidance of trustworthy and invested individuals. By forming a board of directors, you are curating a group of people who are integral to your success and will support you in manifesting the life you truly desire. Embrace transparency and accountability in your interactions with them, and be open to growth and change as you progress on your journey.

As you achieve success and set higher goals, don't hesitate to adapt and expand your board to include new qualified members. This ongoing process will lead to continuous improvement and personal development. Remember, the power of using your board of directors lies in the collaboration and connection with others, fostering a deeper understanding of yourself and your potential for growth.

Keep practicing and integrating this approach into your life, and you'll find yourself empowered to achieve your aspirations and create a more fulfilling reality.

Chapter Nine

Study Guide for Chapter 7, Technique 4: Create a Positive Checkmate

Instructions: Use the information provided in Chapter 7, Technique 4 to answer the following questions and complete the activities. Consider your own beliefs and experiences as you work through each section. Feel free to take notes or reflect on your responses.

Section 1: Introduction to Creating a Positive Checkmate

- <u>Activity 1: Self-Reflection.</u> Reflect on the areas of your life that are most important to you and where you seek to manifest and engage with your desires. Consider the challenges and obstacles you may encounter along the way.

- <u>Activity 2: Learner Choice.</u> Choose one or more of the following activities to further explore the concept of creating a positive checkmate:

  - Visual learner: Create a visual representation (e.g., a flowchart, diagram) that illustrates the steps involved in creating a positive checkmate.

  - Auditory learner: Record yourself explaining the concept of a positive checkmate in your own words and listen to it for reinforcement and reflection.

- Kinesthetic learner: Engage in a physical activity or movement that symbolizes your commitment to creating a positive checkmate (e.g., writing down your goals and physically crossing out the option to quit).

Section 2: Understanding the Concept of Creating a Positive Checkmate

- Explore the concept of a positive checkmate and its application in your life. How does the idea of proactively eliminating the option to quit resonate with you? Write down your thoughts and initial insights.

- <u>Activity 1: Define Your Terms.</u> Create your own definition of "creating a positive checkmate" based on the provided information. Explain the importance of this technique and how it can help you achieve your goals.

- <u>Activity 2: Case Study Analysis.</u> Read or watch a case study of someone who has successfully used a positive checkmate to overcome challenges and achieve their desired outcomes. Analyze their experiences, identifying the strategies they used and the impact on their performance.

Section 3: Identifying Key Allies

- Review the steps outlined in the book on how to create a positive checkmate. Write down the steps in your own words to ensure you have a clear understanding.

- Choose a pathway or area of your life where you want to create a positive checkmate. Identify the key people you will involve in the process—the individuals who are trustworthy, knowledgeable, and have a vested interest in your success.

  ○ Pathway/Area:

  ○ Key Individuals:

- Activity 1: Key Ally Inventory. Identify the people in your life who are most invested in your success and who are likely to notice your progress in the areas you're focusing on. These people should be trustworthy and knowledgeable.

- Activity 2: Stakeholder Interviews. Conduct interviews or conversations with your identified key allies. Discuss your goals and aspirations, and seek their input and advice on how to best approach your manifestation journey.

Section 4: Establishing Transparency and Accountability

- Reflect on the significance of accountability in personal growth and achievement. How does creating a positive checkmate reinforce your sense of accountability? Write down your thoughts and insights.

- Activity 1: Formal Disclosure. Create a plan for how you will disclose your intentions and goals to your key allies. Consider the best method of communication and the information you want to share with them.

- Activity 2: Role-Playing Checkmate Conversation. Role-play a conversation with a friend or partner, where you disclose your intentions and seek their support and accountability. Practice being transparent and open about your goals and plans.

Section 5: Embracing Challenges and Obstacles

- Consider how the checkmate mindset can empower you to navigate challenges and setbacks. How can you cultivate and maintain this mindset throughout your journey? Write down specific strategies or actions you can take.

- Activity 1: Anticipating Roadblocks. Identify potential challenges and obstacles you may encounter on your manifestation journey. Develop strategies for how you will overcome these challenges and stay committed to your goals.

- Activity 2: Positive Affirmations. Create a set of positive affirmations that you can use to motivate yourself during challenging times. These affirmations should reinforce your commitment to your goals and remind you of your accountability.

Section 6: Utilizing the Power of Connection

- Reflect on the four unique ways creating a positive checkmate helps ensure your best performance. How do these benefits resonate with your goals and aspirations? Write down your thoughts and insights.

- Choose one benefit from the list (Burns the Bridges, Ensures Your Best Possible Effort, Utilizes the Power of Two, Deepens Relationships) and explore it further. Discuss how it applies to your chosen pathway and the role it plays in motivating and guiding your actions.

- Activity 1: Leveraging the Power of Two. Explore the concept of invoking a greater presence by connecting with others. Consider how being transparent and accountable to someone else can enhance your motivation and drive.

- Activity 2: Accountability Partner Search. Identify an accountability partner or mentor who can support you in your manifestation journey. Look for someone trustworthy and experienced in the areas you're focusing on.

Section 7: Deepening Relationships Through Accountability

- Write a personal commitment statement outlining your dedication to creating positive checkmates and embracing accountability in your chosen pathway. Include specific actions you will take and a timeline for implementing them.

- Activity 1: Regular Check-In Ritual. Create a plan for regular check-in meetings with your key allies or accountability partner. Discuss your progress, challenges, and any adjustments to your goals or plans.

- Activity 2: Gratitude Journaling. Engage in gratitude journaling to express appreciation for the support and guidance you receive from your key allies. Write about the positive impact their involvement has on your journey.

Section 8: Integrating the Positive Checkmate Approach

- Consider the insights gained from exploring the concept of a positive checkmate and applying it to your chosen pathway. How has this knowledge impacted your perspective and actions?

- Consider future scenarios where you can apply the positive checkmate technique to other areas of your life. Write down potential pathways and individuals you would involve in creating accountability.

- Activity 1: Long-Term Vision. Set long-term goals for how you will continue to create positive checkmates in various aspects of your life. Outline your vision for using accountability to achieve greater success.

- <u>Activity 2: Final Reflection.</u> Conduct a final reflection on your self-study journey of creating a positive checkmate. Write about the growth you've experienced, the connections you've made, and the impact this approach has had on your ability to manifest and engage with your desires.

Conclusion

Congratulations on completing this self-study course on creating a positive checkmate!

You have learned a powerful technique to enhance your commitment to achieving your goals and aspirations by creating transparency and accountability. By involving key allies and mentors, you are empowering yourself to overcome challenges and stay motivated throughout your manifestation journey. Remember, creating a positive checkmate ensures that you remain committed to your success and proactively eliminate the option to quit when faced with obstacles. Continue to leverage the power of connection and deepen your relationships through accountability to cultivate a support system that will drive your progress.

Keep practicing and integrating this approach into your life, and you'll find yourself empowered to achieve your goals and create a positive impact on your reality. Embrace challenges and use the strength of accountability to overcome any barriers on your path to success. You hold the power to transform your life by creating a positive checkmate and taking charge of your destiny. Keep growing, keep learning, and keep manifesting the life you truly desire.

Chapter Ten

Study Guide for Chapter 7, Technique 5: Manifest a Penny

Instructions: Use the information provided in Chapter 7, Technique 5 to answer the following questions and complete the activities. Consider your own beliefs and experiences as you work through each section. Feel free to take notes or reflect on your responses.

Section 1: Introduction to Manifesting a Penny

- Activity 1: Self-Reflection. Reflect on your financial desires and goals. Consider any challenges you may have faced in manifesting money in the past and your current beliefs about abundance and financial success.

- Activity 2: Learner Choice. Choose one or more of the following activities to further explore the concept of manifesting a penny:

  - Visual learner: Create a visual representation (e.g., a collage, vision board) that depicts the energy of abundance and gratitude associated with manifesting a penny.

  - Auditory learner: Record yourself explaining the concept of manifesting a penny and its impact on attracting more money. Listen for reinforcement.

- Kinesthetic learner: Engage in a physical activity (e.g., tossing pennies, creating a jar for manifesting) that embodies the act of manifesting a penny. Reflect on the process and symbolism.

Section 2: Understanding the Concept of Manifesting a Penny

- Reflect on the concept of manifesting a penny and its significance in attracting more money and abundance. How does the idea of intentionally manifesting a penny resonate with you? Write down your thoughts and initial insights.

- <u>Activity 1: Define Your Terms.</u> Create your own definition of "manifesting a penny" based on the provided information. Explain the significance of this technique and its potential impact on your ability to attract abundance.

- <u>Activity 2: Case Study Analysis.</u> Read or watch a case study of someone who has successfully used manifesting a penny (or another symbol) to overcome challenges and achieve their desired outcomes. Analyze their experiences, identifying the strategies they used and the impact on their performance.

Section 3: Intentionally Manifesting a Penny

- Review the steps outlined in the book on how to manifest a penny. Write down the steps in your own words to ensure you have a clear understanding.

- Practice the steps of manifesting a penny in alignment with the situation you chose. Perform the following actions:

  - Step 1: Intentionally manifest a penny by allowing it to be present without actively seeking it. Reflect on your mindset and approach during this process.

- Step 2: Hold the manifested penny in your hand and engage with it. Focus on the symbolism of the penny as a representation of abundance and co-creation.

- Step 3: Express gratitude and celebrate the energy of abundance associated with the manifested penny. Write down or verbalize your own gratitude statements and celebrations.

- Step 4: Carry the raised energy and alignment with financial abundance throughout your day. Notice how it influences your thoughts, actions, and overall perspective on money.

- Activity 1: Penny Hunt. Go on a "penny hunt" in your immediate environment. Look for a penny in a place where you're likely to find one. Practice knowing that a penny is there and discover it with a sense of joy and celebration.

- Activity 2: Symbolic Reflection. Write a reflection on the symbolic meaning of the penny and what it represents in terms of abundance, creativity, and possibility. Consider how this symbolism can enhance your manifesting abilities.

Section 4: Engaging with the Penny's Energy

- Choose a specific situation where you want to manifest more money or financial abundance. Describe the situation and the desired outcome you wish to manifest through the symbolic representation of a penny.

  - Chosen Situation:

  - Desired Outcome:

- Activity 1: Gratitude Practice. Develop a daily gratitude practice where you express thanks for the energy of financial abundance and celebrate the ease of manifestation. Write down affirmations and expressions of gratitude.

- Activity 2: Visualization Exercise. Close your eyes and visualize yourself holding a penny, feeling its weight and substance. Engage with the energy it represents, allowing yourself to embrace the feelings of abundance and ease.

Section 5: Expanding the Practice to Other Desires

- Reflect on the four distinct ways that manifesting a penny helps your performance, as described in the text. How do these benefits resonate with your understanding of attracting abundance and gratitude? Write down your thoughts and insights.

- Reflect on the significance of manifesting a penny in your life and its potential to attract more abundance and gratitude. How does this knowledge impact your perspective on manifesting desired outcomes and embracing an abundance mindset? Write down your thoughts and insights.

- Activity 1: Identify Suitable Tokens. Identify other desires in your life that you can symbolize with easy-to-manifest tokens. For each desire, select a symbol that can be celebrated for its representation of what you wish to manifest.

- Activity 2: Token Manifestation. Practice manifesting the selected tokens for your other desires. Engage with each token based on what it symbolizes, just as you did with the penny. Celebrate and express gratitude for these manifestations.

Section 6: Strengthening Manifesting Efficacy

- Reflect on your experience of manifesting a penny in relation to a chosen situation. How did the process impact your mindset and attitude towards financial abundance? Write down your observations and insights.

- Consider the insights gained from exploring the concept of manifesting a penny and applying it to real-life situations. How do you feel about the potential for attracting more abundance and gratitude through this approach? Write a brief paragraph summarizing your thoughts and any further actions you plan to take to fully embrace this concept.

- <u>Activity 1: Daily Manifesting Ritual.</u> Create a daily manifesting ritual where you intentionally manifest a penny or another token of your choice. Use this practice to build your confidence and strengthen your belief in your manifesting abilities.

- <u>Activity 2: Affirmation Development.</u> Develop a set of affirmations related to your ability to manifest money and other desires effortlessly. Repeat these affirmations daily to reinforce positive beliefs about your manifesting efficacy.

Section 7: Applying Manifesting Skills

- Consider real-life situations to apply this manifesting concept. Choose challenges related to money and abundance that could benefit from this.

    - Situation 1:

    - Situation 2:

    - Situation 3:

- Write a detailed action plan for each situation, outlining the steps you will take to manifest more abundance and gratitude. Include specific actions, strategies, and mindset shifts that align with the concept of manifesting a penny.

    ◦ Action Plan for Situation 1:

    ◦ Action Plan for Situation 2:

    ◦ Action Plan for Situation 3:

- Choose one benefit from the book (easy and repeatable win, authentic celebrations and gratitude, manifesting more money, evergreen practice) and explore it further. Discuss how it manifests in your own experiences of manifesting a penny and the impact it has on your overall well-being and abundance mindset.

- <u>Activity 1: Real-Life Manifestation Goals.</u> Identify specific financial or personal goals you wish to achieve through manifesting. Develop a plan for how you will use the skills you've learned to manifest these goals.

- <u>Activity 2: Progress Tracking.</u> Create a progress tracker to monitor your manifestations and track your successes. Reflect on your growth and improvements in manifesting throughout the self-study course.

Section 8: Integrating Manifesting Skills

- Consider future scenarios where you can actively manifest a penny in different aspects of your life. Write down potential situations and moments where you can embody the concept of manifesting a penny for attracting abundance and gratitude.

- Write a personal commitment statement outlining your dedication to incorporating manifesting a penny into your regular practice. Include specific aspects, situations, and intentions for attracting more abundance and gratitude.

- <u>Activity 1: Long-Term Manifestation Vision.</u> Set long-term goals for how you will continue to practice manifesting in various aspects of your life. Outline your vision for using this technique to attract abundance and achieve your desires.

- <u>Activity 2: Final Reflection.</u> Conduct a final reflection on your self-study journey of manifesting a penny. Write about the transformations you've experienced in your financial beliefs and the impact this approach has had on your ability to attract abundance.

Conclusion:

Congratulations on completing this self-study course on manifesting a penny!

You have learned a powerful technique to shift your financial beliefs, enhance your manifesting abilities, and attract abundance with ease. By engaging with the energy of the penny and celebrating its symbolism, you are aligning yourself with the principles of financial abundance and unlimited creativity.

Manifesting a penny is an evergreen practice that you can apply to attract various desires in your life. Keep practicing and integrating this approach into your daily routine, and you'll find yourself empowered to manifest money and abundance effortlessly. Embrace the energy of gratitude and celebration as you continue to expand your manifesting efficacy. Believe in your ability to attract what you desire, and the Quantum Field will collaborate with you to co-create a reality that aligns with your deepest aspirations.

Keep growing, keep learning, and keep manifesting a life filled with abundance and possibility.

Chapter Eleven

Study Guide for Chapter 7, Technique 6: Use a Positive Affirmation

Instructions: Use the information provided in Chapter 7, Technique 6 to answer the following questions and complete the activities. Consider your own beliefs and experiences as you work through each section. Feel free to take notes or reflect on your responses.

Section 1: Introduction to Positive Affirmations

- Activity 1: Self-Reflection. Reflect on past experiences when you felt off track or lacked confidence in certain areas of your life. Consider how positive affirmations could have been beneficial in those situations.

- Activity 2: Learner Choice. Choose one or more of the following activities to further explore the concept of using a positive affirmation:

  ○ Visual learner: Create a visual representation (e.g., a vision board, collage) that depicts the power of positive affirmations and their impact on personal empowerment.

  ○ Auditory learner: Record yourself reciting positive affirmations that resonate with you. Listen to the recording for reinforcement and reflection.

- Kinesthetic learner: Engage in a physical activity (e.g., writing affirmations, acting out confident postures) that embodies the essence of positive affirmations. Reflect on the experience and identify key insights.

Section 2: Understanding Positive Affirmations

- Reflect on the concept of using positive affirmations and its significance in personal empowerment and boosting confidence. How does the idea of reframing your internal dialogue resonate with you? Write down your thoughts and initial insights.

- <u>Activity 1: Define Positive Affirmations.</u> Create your own definition of "positive affirmations" based on the provided information. Explain the significance of this technique and how it can positively impact your performance.

- <u>Activity 2: Case Study Analysis.</u> Read or watch a case study of someone who has successfully used positive affirmations to boost their confidence and performance. Analyze their experiences, identifying the strategies they used and the impact on their mindset.

Section 3: Crafting Effective Positive Affirmations

- Review the steps outlined in the book on how to use positive affirmations. Write down the steps in your own words to ensure you have a clear understanding.

- Choose a specific situation in your life where you have felt off track or lacking in confidence. Describe the situation and the emotions you experienced.

  - Chosen Situation:

- Emotions Experienced:

- <u>Activity 1: Personal Affirmation Creation.</u> Write three positive affirmations tailored to specific areas of your life where you often feel off track or lack confidence. Ensure these affirmations feel good and are based on authentic beliefs and experiences.

- <u>Activity 2: Believability Assessment.</u> Evaluate the believability of your positive affirmations. Rank them in order of how strongly you believe each one to be true about yourself. Consider adjustments to make the affirmations more believable if necessary.

Section 4: Implementing Positive Affirmations

- Practice the steps of using positive affirmations in relation to a chosen situation. Perform the following actions:

  - Step 1: Identify a positive affirmation that resonates with your situation and emotions. Write it down and reflect on its meaning.

  - Step 2: Repeat the positive affirmation to yourself, focusing on the best-feeling, most believable story about yourself, your abilities, and the situation. Visualize the affirmation as true and empowering.

  - Step 3: Notice any shifts in your emotions and mindset as you engage with the positive affirmation. Reflect on how it helps reframe your internal dialogue and restore your confidence.

  - Step 4: Incorporate the positive affirmation into your daily practice. Repeat it regularly, especially when you feel off track or lacking in confidence.

- Activity 1: Daily Affirmation Practice. Create a daily affirmation practice where you recite your chosen positive affirmations. Choose a time and place conducive to focused reflection and use visualization techniques to reinforce the affirmations.

- Activity 2: Recording and Listening. Record yourself reciting the positive affirmations and listen to the recordings regularly. Observe how hearing your own voice reinforces the beliefs and instills confidence in your abilities.

Section 5: Enhancing Affirmation Efficacy

- Consider real-life situations where you can apply the concept of positive affirmations. Choose specific aspects or challenges in your life where using affirmations can lead to personal empowerment and increased confidence.

  - Situation 1:

  - Situation 2:

  - Situation 3:

- Write a detailed action plan for each situation, outlining the positive affirmations you will use and the steps you will take to reframe your internal dialogue and boost your confidence. Include specific actions, strategies, and mindset shifts that align with the concept of positive affirmations.

  - Action Plan for Situation 1:

  - Action Plan for Situation 2:

- Action Plan for Situation 3:

- <u>Activity 1: Visualization Exercise.</u> Close your eyes and visualize yourself performing successfully in the areas where you usually feel off track or lack confidence. Connect these visualizations to your positive affirmations, reinforcing the alignment between beliefs and desires.

- <u>Activity 2: Gratitude Journal.</u> Start a gratitude journal where you write down things you are grateful for in relation to your abilities and accomplishments. Use this journal to enhance the positive affirmations and recognize your strengths.

Section 6: Integrating Positive Affirmations into Challenging Situations

- Reflect on the four distinct ways that using positive affirmations helps in personal empowerment and confidence, as described in the text. How do these benefits resonate with your understanding of reframing your internal dialogue and building confidence? Write down your thoughts and insights.

- Consider the insights gained from exploring the concept of positive affirmations and applying them to real-life situations. How do you feel about the potential for personal empowerment and increased confidence through this approach? Write a brief paragraph summarizing your thoughts and any further actions you plan to take to fully embrace this concept.

- <u>Activity 1: Role-Play Exercises.</u> Engage in role-play exercises where you put yourself in challenging situations and practice using positive affirmations to restore confidence and focus. Observe how this technique affects your performance and mindset.

- Activity 2: Guided Meditation. Participate in a meditation that incorporates positive affirmations to help you connect with your inner strengths and align your beliefs with your goals. Reflect on the experience and its impact on your confidence.

Section 7: Expanding Positive Affirmations to Other Areas

- Choose one benefit from the book (gets you back on track, inspires action, feels good, helps identify incapable inherited beliefs) and explore it further. Discuss how it manifests in your own experiences of using positive affirmations and the impact it has on your personal empowerment and confidence.

- Reflect on the significance of positive affirmations in your life and their potential to enhance personal empowerment and confidence. How does this knowledge impact your perspective on reframing your internal dialogue and boosting confidence? Write down your thoughts and insights.

- Activity 1: Personalized Affirmation Library. Create a library of positive affirmations tailored to various aspects of your life. Develop affirmations for relationships, career, health, or any other area where you want to boost your confidence and performance.

- Activity 2: Affirmation Visualization Board. Design an affirmation visualization board using images, words, and symbols that represent your goals and beliefs. Display this board in a prominent place to reinforce positive affirmations daily.

Section 8: Long-Term Affirmation Practice

- Consider future scenarios where you can actively use positive affirmations in different aspects of your life. Write down potential situations and moments where reframing your internal dialogue can lead to personal empowerment and increased confidence.

- Write a personal commitment statement outlining your dedication to incorporating positive affirmations into your regular practice. Include specific aspects, situations, and intentions for embracing a positive mindset and cultivating confidence.

- Activity 1: Affirmation Reflection. Reflect on your self-study journey with positive affirmations. Write about the transformations you've experienced in your mindset and performance, and how this technique has empowered you in various aspects of your life.

- Activity 2: Personal Affirmation Mantra. Select one or two most impactful positive affirmations from your library and turn them into a personal mantra. Recite this mantra daily to maintain a positive mindset and strengthen your beliefs.

Conclusion:

Congratulations on completing this self-study course on using positive affirmations for performance enhancement!

You have learned a powerful technique to realign your attitudes and focus onto positive expectations, especially during challenging situations. Positive affirmations serve as reminders of your true beliefs and capabilities, empowering you to get back on track and restore confidence in yourself. By crafting believable and uplifting affirmations, you can inspire positive actions and create a better version of reality for yourself.

Using positive affirmations is an intentional reallocation of your attitudes and focus onto positive expectations that you already possess. It is a tool that can help you navigate through life's challenges and identify any incompatible beliefs or inadequate engagement that may be holding you back. Keep practicing and integrating this approach into your daily routine, and you'll find yourself better equipped to face various situations with confidence and authenticity. Embrace the power of positive self-talk and harness the strength of belief in your abilities.

As you continue your journey, know that you have the capacity to shape your reality and manifest your desires. By consistently using positive affirmations, you are building a solid foundation for a more confident, empowered, and successful self. Keep growing, keep learning, and keep using positive affirmations to create a life filled with positivity, self-assurance, and meaningful accomplishments.

Chapter Twelve

Study Guide for Chapter 7, Technique 7: Make a Manifesting Mount Rushmore

Instructions: Use the information provided in Chapter 7, Technique 7 to answer the following questions and complete the activities. Consider your own beliefs and experiences as you work through each section. Feel free to take notes or reflect on your responses.

Section 1: Introduction to Making a Manifesting Mount Rushmore

- <u>Activity 1: Self-Reflection.</u> Reflect on areas of your life where you have struggled to manifest your desires as you truly want. Consider the impact of collaboration and interdependence on achieving your goals.

- <u>Activity 2: Learner Choice.</u> Choose one or more of the following activities to further explore the concept of making a manifesting Mount Rushmore:

  - Visual learner: Create a visual representation (e.g., a collage, vision board) that depicts the four interconnected accomplishments you would choose for your manifesting Mount Rushmore.

  - Auditory learner: Record yourself explaining the concept of making a manifesting Mount Rushmore and its significance in your own words. Listen to it for reinforcement and reflection.

- Kinesthetic learner: Engage in a physical activity (e.g., sculpting, crafting) to create miniature representations of the four accomplishments you would choose for your manifesting Mount Rushmore. Reflect on the process and symbolism.

Section 2: Understanding Making a Manifesting Mount Rushmore

- Reflect on the concept of making a manifesting Mount Rushmore in important areas of your life. How does the idea of selecting four interconnected accomplishments resonate with you? Write down your thoughts and initial insights.

- Activity 1: Define Making a Manifesting Mount Rushmore. Create your own definition of "Making a Manifesting Mount Rushmore" based on the provided information. Explain the significance of this technique and how it can enhance your manifestation process.

- Activity 2: Case Study Analysis. Read or watch a case study of someone who has successfully used the technique of Making a Manifesting Mount Rushmore to manifest their desires. Analyze their experiences and identify the strategies they employed for success.

Section 3: Identifying Desired States of Being

- Review the steps outlined in the book on how to make a manifesting Mount Rushmore. Write down the steps in your own words for a clear understanding.

- Choose an important aspect of your life where you want to manifest a desired state of being. Determine the broad desire and articulate it as a state of being rather than a specific accomplishment.

  ○ Chosen Aspect:

  ○ Desired State of Being:

- Activity 1: Personal Manifestation Goals. Identify the most important areas of your life where you want to manifest your desires differently. Choose broad states of being that represent your overall desires (e.g., wealth, love, health).

- Activity 2: Visualization Exercise. Close your eyes and visualize yourself experiencing the desired states of being you have identified. Connect with the emotions and sensations associated with achieving these goals.

Section 4: Selecting Four Accomplishments

- Identify and select four interconnected accomplishments that will collectively evoke a desired state of being. These accomplishments will be the giant, sculpted heads on your manifesting Mount Rushmore.

  ○ Accomplishment 1:

  ○ Accomplishment 2:

  ○ Accomplishment 3:

  ○ Accomplishment 4:

- <u>Activity 1: Accomplishment Brainstorming.</u> Brainstorm and list four specific accomplishments for each desired state of being you've chosen. These accomplishments should collectively evoke that state of being.

- <u>Activity 2: Believability Assessment.</u> Evaluate the believability of each of the four accomplishments you have listed. Rank them in order of how strongly you believe each one will help you manifest your desired state of being.

Section 5: Intentional Manifestation Techniques

- Develop a plan to intentionally manifest each of the four accomplishments you've selected. Explore different techniques and approaches that align with each accomplishment. Consider learning from people who have successfully manifested similar accomplishments.

  - Accomplishment 1 Techniques:

  - Accomplishment 2 Techniques:

  - Accomplishment 3 Techniques:

  - Accomplishment 4 Techniques:

- Dedicate at least 150 minutes per week (and more if possible) to actively manifesting each of the four accomplishments. Practice the recommended techniques and strategies for each accomplishment.

  - Weekly Time Commitment:

- Activity 1: Applying Manifestation Techniques. Apply the manifestation techniques you have learned earlier in this course to intentionally manifest each of the four accomplishments. Use visualization, gratitude practices, and positive affirmations to strengthen your belief in their attainment.

- Activity 2: Tracking Progress. Create a progress tracker to record your efforts and achievements in manifesting each of the four accomplishments. Monitor your progress regularly and celebrate small victories along the way.

Section 6: Collaborative Manifestation

- Reflect on the four distinct ways that making a manifesting Mount Rushmore helps your performance, as described in the text. How do these benefits resonate with your understanding of personal growth and success? Write down your thoughts and insights.

- Choose one benefit from the list (spreading the wealth, distributing the responsibilities, lowering the pressure, mirroring how you manifest reality) and explore it further. Discuss how it manifests in your own experiences of making a manifesting Mount Rushmore and the impact it has on your overall well-being and performance.

- Activity 1: Seek Support and Collaboration. Identify individuals or groups who can provide support and collaboration in manifesting each of the four accomplishments. Reach out to mentors, friends, or colleagues who can offer guidance and assistance.

- Activity 2: Collaborative Visualization. Engage in collaborative visualization exercises with your support network. Visualize yourselves collectively achieving the desired state of being and celebrating your accomplishments together.

Section 7: Balancing Responsibilities and Pressure

- Reflect on the insights gained from exploring the concept of making a manifesting Mount Rushmore and applying it to real-life situations. How do you feel about the potential for personal growth and success through this approach? Write a brief paragraph summarizing your thoughts and any further actions you plan to take to fully embrace this concept.

- Consider real-life situations where you can apply the concept of making a manifesting Mount Rushmore. Choose specific aspects or challenges in your life that could benefit from this approach.

    - Situation 1:

    - Situation 2:

    - Situation 3:

- Write a detailed action plan for each situation, outlining the steps you will take to manifest each of the four interconnected accomplishments attached to each situation. Include specific actions, strategies, and mindset shifts that align with each accomplishment.

    - Action Plan for Situation 1:

    - Action Plan for Situation 2:

    - Action Plan for Situation 3:

- Activity 1: Responsibility Allocation. Reflect on how you can distribute responsibilities equally among the four accomplishments on a manifesting Mount Rushmore. Consider how each accomplishment complements and supports the others.

- Activity 2: Pressure Reduction Techniques. Explore strategies to lower the pressure and stress associated with manifesting your desires. Practice mindfulness, meditation, or relaxation techniques to maintain a sense of calm and focus.

Section 8: Integrating Making a Manifesting Mount Rushmore into Daily Life

- Consider the significance of making a manifesting Mount Rushmore in the important areas of your life. How does this knowledge impact your perspective on personal growth, success, and manifesting desired states of being? Write down your thoughts and insights.

- Consider future scenarios where you can actively make a manifesting Mount Rushmore in different aspects of your life. Write down potential situations and moments where you can embody the concept of manifesting interconnected accomplishments for personal growth and success.

- Write a personal commitment statement outlining your dedication to incorporating making a manifesting Mount Rushmore into your regular practice. Include specific aspects, situations, and intentions for personal growth and success.

- Activity 1: Daily Manifesting Ritual. Create a daily manifesting ritual where you visualize your desired state of being and affirm your commitment to manifesting each of the four accomplishments on your Mount Rushmore.

- Activity 2: Long-Term Goal Setting. Set long-term goals for each of the four accomplishments and create actionable plans to achieve them. Break down the steps needed to reach each goal and monitor your progress regularly.

Conclusion:

Congratulations on completing this self-study course on Making a Manifesting Mount Rushmore for maximum success!

You have learned a powerful technique to manifest your desires more effectively by leveraging collaboration and interdependence. By selecting four significant accomplishments that collectively evoke your desired state of being, you spread the wealth, distribute responsibilities, and reduce pressure on any single achievement.

Manifesting is a dance between you and the one consciousness. You get to lead the way by providing intentional actions to evoke your desired states of being. As you intentionally manifest each of the four accomplishments on your Mount Rushmore, remember the power of belief, visualization, and collaboration.

By integrating the principles and techniques of Making a Manifesting Mount Rushmore into your daily life, you empower yourself to achieve your goals with greater ease and success. Embrace the journey of intentional manifestation, and continue to focus on your strengths and passions. You have the capacity to shape your reality and manifest your desires. Keep growing, keep learning, and keep collaborating to create a life filled with abundance, fulfillment, and meaningful accomplishments.

Chapter Thirteen

Study Guide for Chapter 7, Technique 8: Create a Flow State

Instructions: Use the information provided in Chapter 7, Technique 8 to answer the following questions and complete the activities. Consider your own beliefs and experiences as you work through each section. Feel free to take notes or reflect on your responses.

Section 1: Introduction to Creating a Flow State

- Activity 1: Self-Reflection. Reflect on times in your life when you have experienced a flow state. Consider how being in the flow state enhanced your performance and connection to the present moment.

- Activity 2: Learner Choice. Choose one or more of the following activities to further explore the concept of creating a flow state:

  - Visual learner: Create a visual representation (e.g., a collage, mind map) that illustrates the elements and benefits of a flow state.

  - Auditory learner: Record yourself explaining the concept of a flow state and its significance in your own words. Listen to it for reinforcement and reflection.

- Kinesthetic learner: Engage in a physical activity that allows you to experience a state of flow (e.g., painting, playing a musical instrument) and reflect on your experience afterward.

Section 2: Understanding the Flow State

- Reflect on the concept of a flow state and its potential impact on your personal growth and connection with the Quantum Field. How does the idea of losing yourself in the moment resonate with you? Write down your thoughts and initial insights.

- Activity 1: Define the Flow State. Create your own definition of the flow state based on the provided information. Explain the significance of being in the flow state and how it can positively impact your manifestation and engagement with reality.

- Activity 2: Case Study Analysis. Read or watch a case study of someone who has successfully experienced flow states and achieved exceptional performance. Analyze their experiences and identify common factors that contribute to entering a flow state.

Section 3: Selecting a Challenging Physical Activity

- Review the steps outlined in the book on how to create a flow state. Write down the steps in your own words to ensure you have a clear understanding.

- Choose a challenging physical activity that you would like to engage in to create a flow state. Consider both exercise-related and non-workout-related options. This activity should require physical engagement and present a challenge.

  ○ Chosen Activity:

- Explore resources (e.g., trainers, experts, videos) related to the chosen activity to learn the best form and techniques for performing it. Take notes on proper form and engage in practice sessions to develop your skill level.

  ○ Resources:

- <u>Activity 1: Your Chosen Activity.</u> You've selected an activity that you are passionate enough about and that requires physical engagement. Consider the benefits of engaging in this activity for flow state induction.

- <u>Activity 2: Learning Proper Form.</u> You've researched and learned the best form for performing the chosen physical activity. What advice and guidance from experts or experienced practitioners ensure you are following proper techniques? And in what ways does their expertise help you follow it?

Section 4: Creating Flow States through Practice

- Dedicate at least 150 minutes per week to engaging in the chosen activity while giving your best effort to follow the learned form. Remember that consistency and progress over time are key to creating more frequent and powerful flow states.

  ○ Weekly Time Commitment:

- Activity 1: Setting a Practice Schedule. Create a weekly practice schedule for your chosen physical activity, aiming for at least 150 minutes per week. Divide the time into daily increments that suit your lifestyle.

- Activity 2: Developing Skill Level. Give your best effort to follow the learned form during each practice session. Focus on improving your skill level and challenging yourself to go deeper into giving a whole-self effort of mind, body, and energy.

Section 5: Recognizing Flow State Indicators

- Reflect on the five characteristics of being in a flow state described in the text. How do these characteristics resonate with your understanding of being fully present and connected? Write down your thoughts and insights.

- Choose one characteristic from the list of 4 in the book (100 percent focus, losing your self, time disappearance, deep connections, energy flow) and explore it further. Discuss how it manifests in your own flow state experiences and the impact it has on your overall well-being and performance.

- Activity 1: Identifying Flow State Characteristics. Study the characteristics of being in a flow state, such as heightened focus, time distortion, and a feeling of connection with the universe. Practice recognizing these indicators during your physical activity.

- Activity 2: Mindfulness Exercise. Engage in a mindfulness exercise while performing your chosen activity. Focus on being fully present in the moment, observe your thoughts, and let go of distractions.

Section 6: Processing Emotions in the Flow State

- Consider how a flow state can help you process and explore your emotions. How can you utilize this state to follow painful feelings back to their source and uncover inadequate beliefs and engagement patterns? Write down specific strategies or actions you can take.

- <u>Activity 1: Emotional Processing Practice.</u> While in a flow state, allow yourself to feel and process any emotions that arise. Practice nonjudgmental immersion in your feelings and ask yourself, "What must I believe about myself to feel this way?"

- <u>Activity 2: Tracing Emotions to Beliefs.</u> Follow painful feelings back to their source by exploring the beliefs and thought patterns that underlie them. Identify any limiting beliefs and make note of them for possible use with the belief raising process.

Section 7: Direct Communication with the Quantum Field

- Write a personal commitment statement outlining your dedication to incorporating flow states into your regular practice. Include specific activities, time commitments, and intentions for personal growth and connection.

- Reflect on the insights gained from exploring the concept of a flow state and applying it to your chosen activity. How do you feel about the potential for personal connection and growth through flow states? Write a brief paragraph summarizing your thoughts and any further actions you plan to take to fully embrace flow state experiences.

- Activity 1: Flow State Communication. During a flow state, practice communicating with the Quantum Field (the one consciousness). Develop your ability to receive personal and nonjudgmental feedback from the universe.

- Activity 2: Asking Empowering Questions. Utilize the direct communication with the Quantum Field to ask empowering questions about your life, reality, and engagement. Seek guidance and perspective to inform your decision-making.

Section 8: Integrating Flow State in Daily Life

- Consider future scenarios where you can intentionally create flow states in different areas of your life. Write down potential activities and moments where you can immerse yourself in a state of flow for personal connection and growth.

- Reflect on the significance of creating a flow state for personal growth, connection with the Quantum Field, and the potential for high-quality solutions. How does this knowledge impact your perspective on intentional manifesting? Write down your thoughts and insights.

- Activity 1: Flow State Integration. Incorporate flow state practices into your daily routine. Continue to engage in the chosen physical activity and strive to create flow states regularly.

- Activity 2: Reflection and Journaling. Reflect on your experiences with flow states and record your insights in a journal. Document the solutions and guidance you receive during flow state communication.

Conclusion:

Congratulations on completing the self-study course on Creating a Flow State for personalized help and maximum performance!

You have learned a powerful technique to intentionally enter the flow state, connect with the Quantum Field, and achieve exceptional performance in various areas of your life. By engaging in challenging physical activities, learning proper form, and giving your best effort during practice, you position yourself for flow state induction. In the flow state, you can experience heightened focus, time distortion, and a sense of connection with the universe.

Additionally, the flow state enables you to process emotions, trace them back to limiting beliefs, and receive high-quality solutions and guidance from the Quantum Field.

As you continue to integrate flow state practices into your daily life, remember the importance of an autotelic focus—a mindset focused on learning, growth, and change. Embrace the process of engaging with your reality, knowing that you are not alone in this journey. The Quantum Field is always available to provide personalized assistance and direction.

Embrace the flow state as a powerful tool to manifest your desires, enhance your performance, and cultivate a deep connection with the present moment. By creating a flow state, you put the Quantum Field on your board of directors, allowing for personal transformation and alignment with your desires.

Stay committed to your practice, stay open to learning and growth, and continue to engage with reality from a place of authenticity and vulnerability. As you master the art of creating a flow state, you empower yourself to co-create the life you truly desire—one that is filled with joy, abundance, and fulfillment.

Chapter Fourteen

Study Guide for Chapter 8: How Greg Intentionally Manifests and Engages with His Reality

Instructions: Use the information provided in Chapter 8 to answer the following questions and complete the activities. Consider your own beliefs and experiences as you work through each section. Feel free to take notes or reflect on your responses.

Section 1: Reflecting on Opportunities

- What does it mean to manifest wealth, health, love, and other desires in your life?

- How can taking advantage of opportunities lead to creating the outcomes you truly want?

- In what ways have you experienced the benefits of giving your best effort in various situations?

- Take a moment to consider the idea that every moment presents opportunities to manifest wealth, health, love, and anything else you desire. How does this perspective make you feel? Do you feel empowered and excited about the possibilities?

- Think about times when you've faced dissatisfying situations in your life. What were your typical responses to those challenges? Were you focused on blaming yourself or others, or were you open to examining how you engage with reality?

- <u>Activity 1: Reflection Questions.</u> Consider the following questions:

  - What does the concept of "opportunities" mean to you?

  - How do you perceive the relationship between opportunities and the outcomes you desire?

  - Have you experienced moments when you've taken advantage of opportunities to create the outcomes you want? Describe those experiences.

- <u>Activity 2: Daily Opportunity Journal.</u> Keep a journal for one week where you record the opportunities you encounter each day. Reflect on how you engaged with these opportunities and the outcomes they led to. Identify any patterns or areas for improvement in your approach to daily opportunities.

Section 2: Identifying Limiting Beliefs

- Why is it essential to align your beliefs with your desires when engaging with reality?

- How can intentionally manifesting your desires help you create more aligned versions of reality?

- Share an experience where aligning your beliefs with your desires positively impacted your engagement with reality.

- Reflect on an area of your life where you feel dissatisfied or stuck. What are the beliefs you hold about this aspect of your reality? Write them down without judgment or filtering.

- Consider how these beliefs might be affecting your experiences and outcomes in this area. Are they supporting you in manifesting the reality you desire, or are they holding you back?

- <u>Activity 1: Mindful Engagement.</u> Practice being fully present in the moment, focusing on the tasks at hand without getting lost in future results. How does this practice impact your ability to align with opportunities and take intentional action?

- <u>Activity 2: Vibrational Alignment.</u> Each morning, set aside time to align yourself vibrationally with the opportunities of the day. How does this practice influence your mindset and emotional state throughout the day?

Section 3: Embracing Responsibility for Fulfillment

- What is the difference between accepting responsibility for fulfillment and blaming yourself for challenges?

- How can accepting responsibility for your fulfillment empower you to make positive changes in your life?

- Share an experience where accepting responsibility for your fulfillment led to a positive shift in your reality.

- Explore the idea of accepting responsibility for your fulfillment. How does this concept differ from blaming yourself for any pain or challenges you face? How does it feel to prioritize your fulfillment over external success or achievements?

- How might embracing responsibility for your fulfillment impact the way you approach challenges and opportunities in your life?

- Activity 1: The Fulfillment Mindset. Write down three challenging situations in your life and identify how you can accept responsibility for your fulfillment in each case. Outline actionable steps you can take to manifest fulfilling versions of reality in those situations.

- Activity 2: Empowering Affirmations. Create a list of empowering affirmations related to accepting responsibility for your fulfillment. Repeat these affirmations daily and observe how they influence your mindset and actions.

Section 4: Seeking Expert Mentorship

- What does it mean to align yourself vibrationally with the opportunities provided in each moment?

- How can you prioritize effort over specific outcomes in your daily life?

- Describe a situation where you experienced the power of being vibrationally aligned with an opportunity.

- Reflect on the importance of seeking mentorship from individuals who have achieved verifiable success in the areas you want to improve. Have you actively sought mentorship from experts in your life?

- How might learning from these experts help you in your journey of intentional manifesting and engagement?

- Activity 1: Identifying Mentors. Identify individuals who you consider to be experts in areas you wish to improve. These mentors can be authors, speakers, professionals, or anyone whose success you admire. Research their achievements and the strategies they use to manifest their desires.

- Activity 2: Learning from Mentors. Choose one of your identified mentors and study their methods and teachings. How can you apply their insights to your life? Implement one of their suggestions and document the changes you observe.

Section 5: Applying the Metaphor of Running

- Why is giving your best effort in each moment crucial for intentional manifesting?

- How can focusing on effort rather than outcomes lead to better results and reduced performance anxiety?

- Share a personal experience where putting forth your best effort positively influenced the outcome.

- Consider the metaphor of running as a way to channel information from the Quantum Field. How does this metaphor resonate with your own experiences of seeking flow states or creative inspiration?

- Think about the importance of giving your best effort in each moment, rather than focusing solely on performance outcomes. How might this shift in focus impact your approach to achieving your desires?

- Activity 1: Running Reflection. Reflect on a physical activity or hobby you enjoy. How can you see it as a metaphor for intentional manifesting and engaging with reality? What lessons can you draw from this activity to apply to other aspects of your life?

- Activity 2: Visualization Exercise. Close your eyes and visualize yourself running with the same dedication and focus as Greg Kuhn does. Imagine how this mindset and effort translate into other areas of your life. How does this exercise influence your motivation to manifest your desires?

Section 6: Mastering Each Step of Manifesting

- Describe the significance of mastering each step of manifesting your desires.

- Share an example from your life where mastering a foundational step led to better results in a subsequent step.

- How can breaking down your desires into smaller steps help you maintain focus and progress?

- Imagine your desires as a series of steps to be mastered, much like learning to ride a horse. Identify the first step you need to take to move closer to your desires. What is it, and how might you approach mastering it?

- How can focusing on mastering each step, rather than fixating on the end result, help you stay present and committed to giving your best effort?

- Activity 1: Manifesting Goals. Identify a specific desire or goal you wish to manifest. Break it down into smaller steps or milestones, just like Greg does when learning to ride a horse. What is the first step you need to master to manifest your desire?

- Activity 2: Taking Action. Take action towards mastering the first step of manifesting your desire. Keep a journal to track your progress and any feedback or insights you gain from the experience.

Section 7: Recognizing Current Manifestation

- How can you treat every outcome as a formative assessment and use it to learn and grow?

- Share an experience where you learned valuable lessons from a less-than-desired outcome.

- How does adopting a growth mindset enhance your ability to manifest your desires intentionally?

- Embrace the idea that you are currently manifesting all your desires to the best of your ability. What areas of your life are you intentionally manifesting and engaging with at this moment?

- Acknowledge the importance of recognizing your efforts and progress, even as you work towards bigger aspirations. How might this mindset impact your motivation and growth?

- Activity 1: Celebrating Effort. Celebrate your efforts in manifesting your desire, regardless of the immediate outcomes. Write down three positive aspects of your current progress and acknowledge how your best effort is moving you closer to your goals.

- Activity 2: Formative Assessment. Shift your perspective on outcomes from being final judgments to formative assessments. How does this perspective allow you to view each experience as an opportunity to learn and grow?

Section 8: The Driving Force Behind Your Intentional Manifesting

- How does embracing the journey of intentional manifesting contribute to your overall fulfillment?

- Share your thoughts on staking a claim for manifesting your desires right from the start.

- How can recognizing your efforts in the present moment enhance your capacity for intentional manifestation?

- Reflect on the driving force behind your decision to intentionally manifest and engage with your reality. How do aligning your beliefs, seizing opportunities, and performing to the best of your ability contribute to your sense of fulfillment?

- How might embracing the inevitability of public-facing performances motivate you to give your best effort and align with opportunities that come your way?

- Activity 1: Personal Desires. Identify and write down your current personal desires, just as Greg does for himself. Reflect on how these desires drive you to intentionally manifest and engage with your reality.

- Activity 2: Affirming Commitment. Write a personal commitment statement, affirming your dedication to intentional manifesting and engaging with reality. Read this statement aloud each morning to reinforce your focus and motivation.

Conclusion:

Congratulations on completing this self-study course for Chapter 8 of A Handbook for Those Already Born!

You've explored the power of intentional manifesting and engagement, recognizing that each moment presents opportunities for growth and fulfillment. Embrace the journey of learning, growing, and changing as you align your beliefs, seize opportunities, and give your best effort in each moment.

You are the driving force behind your reality, and by focusing on your effort and growth, you can manifest the life you truly desire. Keep channeling your creative inspiration, and may your intentional manifesting lead you to experiences of joy, success, and fulfillment. You've got this!

About the Author

Greg Kuhn is a Manifesting Coach, specializing in manifesting the big stuff! Successful health, fitness, wealth, family, marriage, career, and relationships are all examples of what Greg focuses on - your most important desires. To contact Greg, visit his website: www.ManifesttheBigStuff.com

A professional educator, coach, writer, speaker, and podcaster, Greg has been teaching people how to change their beliefs and manifest the reality they truly desire since 2013. Using a method forged in the fires of personal and professional disaster, Greg teaches you how to lead your subconscious (by speaking its native tongue) to change the reality you manifest. And he shows you how to sit in the captain's chair, assuming your role as the CEO of your life. Which all results in truly aligning your beliefs, engaging more successfully with reality, and finally manifesting your most important desires.

Watch Greg's podcast, Manifest the Big Stuff, along with other life-changing content, on his YouTube Channel: https://www.youtube.com/@manifestthebigstuff

And listen to Manifest the Big Stuff on Apple Podcasts, Spotify, Google Podcasts, Stitcher, and almost anywhere else you can listen to podcasts.

Engage with Greg via the links below:

Greg's Free Facebook Manifesting Group: https://www.facebook.com/groups/manifestthebigstuff

Greg's Free Quantum Thoughts Newsletter: https://manifestthebigstuff.com/newsletter/

Book Greg to Speak at Your Event: https://manifestthebigstuff.com/speaking/

Greg's LinkedIn: https://www.linkedin.com/in/greg-kuhn-a058913a/

Greg's Twitter: @KuhnGregory

Greg's Instagram: @gregoryskuhn1967

ALSO BY GREG KUHN

Why Quantum Physicists Don't Get Fat

Learn how to see yourself, your body, and your reality in new ways that help you gain the body you desire! Available in paperback and Kindle from Amazon.

Why Quantum Physicists Do Not Fail

Using everyday language and "street-level" instructions, this book will have you back on track in no time! Available in paperback and Kindle from Amazon and as an audiobook from Audible.

Why Quantum Physicists Do Not Suffer

Learn a great secret you can start using right now to minimize, or even end, your suffering! Available in Kindle from Amazon and as an audiobook from Audible.

Why Quantum Physicists Create More Abundance

What does science say about the law of attraction? Is it real? Can it be explained or verified? Yes! Available in Kindle from Amazon and as an audiobook from Audible.

How Quantum Physicists Build New Beliefs

By learning to speak your subconscious' native tongue, you will truly grow your beliefs into alignment with your desires! Available in paperback and Kindle from Amazon and as an audiobook from Audible.

Why Quantum Physicists Play "Grow a Greater You"

By turning to new paradigms from Quantum Physics, Greg has forged a simple, but powerful, roadmap to manifest reality as you truly desire! Available in paperback and Kindle from Amazon and as an audiobook from Audible.

The 30-Minute Soulmate

Whether you're in a relationship now or not, you will find solutions as you learn to manifest, and be, a soulmate! Available in paperback and Kindle from Amazon.